Praise for *Educational*

"Some education books are dry. They're a chore to read, and it's hard to see oneself in them. This is not one of those books. This is a book about educational technology, but it's also a book about tater tot casserole, ramen noodles, and beards. Jake Miller doesn't take himself too seriously, but that doesn't mean that his tips, wisdom, and inspiration won't change you as an educator. You'll fly through this book and enjoy the journey. And you'll be a better educator because of it."

—Matt Miller, author, *Ditch That Textbook*

"Jake Miller has done it. He has found a way to help teachers easily understand how they can create truly powerful learning experiences for their students using the *right* technology! This book is entertaining, helpful, and packed full of really inspiring ideas. This should be on the desk of every teacher! It will serve as an incredible resource that you will go back to over and over again! Buy this for yourself and every teacher you know!"

—Holly Clark, author, blogger, speaker

"Enjoyable stories, thoughtful analogies, and witty wisecracks are exactly what I expect from Jake Miller, and this book delivers! The intriguing chapter titles draw me in, and each chapter's checklist is handy for keeping track of what I want to try. And yes, Jake asks you to write inside this book (and you really should). Jake has done the research, and I appreciate his open and honest comparisons of tools. I also appreciate how he explains his systematic approach to solving problems."

—Tony Vincent, educator

"If you think this is the same old, boring teaching book—you're wrong! Jake has a unique style and humor that will have you talking about how edtech, fashion, and tater tots can work together to change teaching and learning. Inside this book, you will find great tips, fantastic edtech tools, powerful instructional strategies, and a whole heap of quirky humor! Buy this book. (You can thank me later.)"

—Kasey Bell, author, podcaster, and international speaker
at ShakeUpLearning.com

"No matter what goal you have in your classroom, Jake has dozens of tools to help you teach and your students learn. Most importantly, *Educational Duct Tape* will help you choose the best resource to meet your needs, with equal parts inspiration, humor, and practicality."

—Eric Curts, educator, author, speaker

"As a long-time listener to *EduDuctTape*, I have been following Jake's work for a while. Very similar to his style on the podcast, Jake continues to draw readers in with his personable and humorous nature. He supports anecdotes with actionable steps and opportunities for reflection that make this book a fun and informative read."

—**Sarah Thomas, PhD**, regional tech coordinator, #EduMatch Founder/CEO

"Education is one 'make it work' moment after another (hence the need for duct tape)! Technology can be incredibly useful, yet the sheer volume of educational technology tools is daunting. In this engaging book, Jake Miller guides teachers through an exploration of technology tools to help them develop more confidence in their selection and use of technology to meet the needs of their students. It isn't about the number of tools you use; it's how you use them that matters!"

—**Catlin R. Tucker, EdD**, educator, international trainer, keynote speaker and bestselling author

"Jake's book is full of edtech tools and activity ideas for teachers looking to use technology in their classrooms. This book has suggestions for teachers who are brand-new to technology integration and those looking to up their game with edtech this school year."

—**Monica Burns, EdD**, author of *EdTech Essentials*

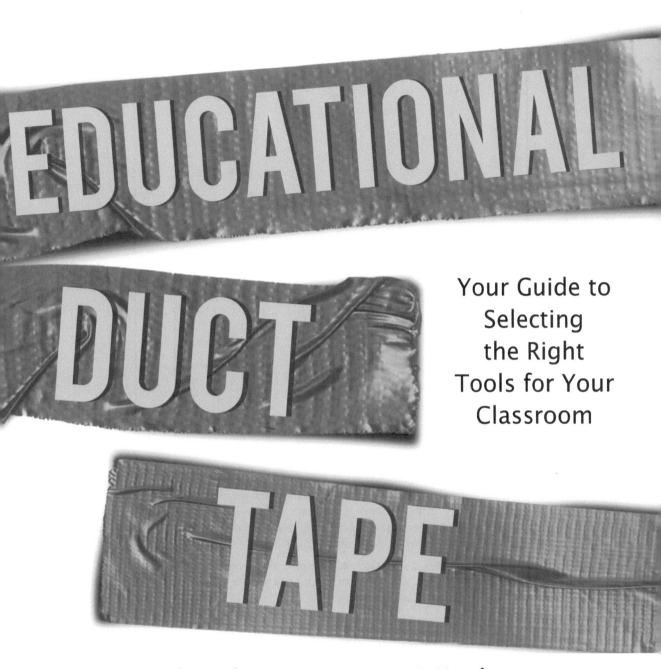

EDUCATIONAL DUCT TAPE

Your Guide to Selecting the Right Tools for Your Classroom

An EdTech Integration Mindset

JAKE MILLER

Published by Jake Miller Educational Opportunities, LLC

Editing and Interior Design by My Writers' Connection
Cover design by Genesis Kohler

Paperback ISBN: 979-8-9876070-0-8
eBook ISBN: 979-8-9876070-1-5

This book is dedicated to . . .

The school psychologist. Behind every great book are the people who make sacrifices to help the author make it happen. I never could have done this without your support and patience! I love you, April!

And to Cohen Bear, Peanut, and LG for always cheering me on! I can't wait to read the books that you three write someday!

And to my parents, Lynn and Kathy, for teaching me that I can do whatever I put my mind to!

CONTENTS

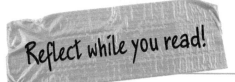
Reflect while you read!

Access and print your free copy of the Educational
Duct Tape: An EdTech Integration Mindset Workbook at
JakeMiller.net/EduDuctTape-Workbook!

ONE

A BOOK ABOUT CONTEMPORARY FASHION TRENDS

SUMMER 2018

This is a book about contemporary fashion. Fashion in the year 2018—the year I started drafting this book—from the eyes of a thirty-eight-year-old man. A book that, I'm sure, you are eager to read. A book I have dreamed of writing all my life.

Here are some fashion *Don'ts* for you from 2018:

MEN	WOMEN
Don't wear sweatpants with elastic at the ankles.	**Don't** wear athletic wear outside of the gym.
Don't wear brightly colored athletic shoes.	**Don't** wear high-waisted mom jeans.
Don't wear your hat with a flat brim.	**Don't** wear crop-top shirts.

2021

Ugh. All of the *don'ts* I listed when I started writing this book are now outdated. Half of the girls in middle school wear workout pants and the other half wear high-waisted jeans. Half of the boys wear "joggers" that look too short for them and their hat brims are as flat as a board.

Writing a book about contemporary fashion is tough because fashions change faster than authors can write or publishers can publish.

So instead, I will write a book about educational technology.

Summer 2018

Here are some educational technology tips for Summer 2018:

- Use Recap to have your students respond with videos because the best features of Flipgrid are in the paid version.

- Use a tool other than Google Classroom for grading your assignments with rubrics and recording grades because those features aren't available in Google Classroom.
- Ignore the tool called Google Hangouts that's in your Google account. You'll never need it.
- Use Kahoot to host a fun review session for your students.

2021

Ugh. All of the edtech tips I listed are now outdated. Recap no longer exists, and Flipgrid is now 100 percent free. Google Classroom now has a gradebook and rubrics. Google Meet (formerly Google Hangouts) and Zoom became the most relevant tech tools of 2020 and 2021 (*Thanks a lot, 'Rona!*). Kahoot is still a good tool, but Blooket, Gimkit, and others now deserve mention as popular classroom review game tools.

Writing a book about ~~contemporary fashion~~ *educational technology* is tough because ~~fashions~~ *edtech tools* change faster than authors can write and publishers can publish.

To prove this point (and give you a chance to laugh at me), let's look at a brief history of fashion and edtech trends from my own life.

1986

FASHION: Oh geez. Thanks for putting me in this shirt, Mom.

Photo Credit: Olan Mills Portraits, I assume

EDTECH: *Ahhhh,* the smell of fresh Ditto worksheets! Should I be concerned about how much I liked the scent of the alcohol-based fluid that created these worksheets!?

1988

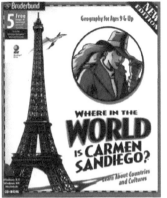

FASHION: Wow. Just wow. That hair. That outfit.

EDTECH: Sorry, I couldn't pick just one! Neither was brand-new in 1988, but this is when I experienced the wonders of the Oregon Trail and Carmen Sandiego games.

1995

FASHION: Oh man. Now that's a sweet turtleneck. And paired with that flannel shirt?

EDTECH: Newer versions of HyperStudio are still out there—and potentially useful. This version, which I used in a high school course, was likely my only experience with creating digitally as a student in a K–12 classroom.

2001

FASHION: An unfortunate Mark McGrath–influenced phase. And why wear T-shirts under unbuttoned dress shirts?

EDTECH: PowerPoint in 2001? About as cool as my "frosted tips" hairstyle.

2005

FASHION: Ashton Kutcher convinced me to grow my hair out and wear my dad's old Miller High Life shirt.

EDTECH: My mom convinced me to attend a SMART Board training and it changed everything (except for my hair).

2014

FASHION: Being a dad? Always in fashion.

EDTECH: Folders upon folders of student Google Docs? Not always in fashion.

2021

FASHION: That's me now. Is it possible that one day I'll look back regretfully at my style?

EDTECH: There are too many amazing edtech tools to just show one!

I could dedicate all of the pages in this book to telling you about the best educational technology tools available to you and your students, but it would be outdated before the ink dried. If I pack it with screenshots of how to use Google Classroom, Flipgrid, or Nearpod, my book would be in the clearance rack as soon as it's released. Technology evolves quickly and edtech changes. Fast.

And it's overwhelming.

That's why I'm here to help. Not by telling you what fashio—*er*, educational technologies to choose, but by telling you *how* to choose them. While I will share specific tools, and I may even throw in a screenshot or two, no current edtech tool will be the focus of this book. My goal is to help you navigate the rapidly evolving educational technology landscape so you are always equipped to make the best choice for you.

I will share how to use some tools to achieve certain goals or meet specific needs, but please remember that you are reading this book for you (and maybe for your students' benefit too). There may be sections about goals that don't apply to you. I may discuss tools that aren't right for you. So you may choose to skip those sections. (*You have my permission to do so.*)

Before you decide what to skip, however, you need to know where you're trying to go. You need to calibrate your compass. I'd like to help you do that so you can find *your* north star for educational technology integration.

You'll never learn to use all of the tools, or worse yet, actually use all of them. And even if you could, you shouldn't. No single technology is the right tool for every educator, classroom, content, and group of students. The best thing you can do is know how to make decisions about *which ones* to learn and integrate into your classroom for the benefit of you and your students.

And how will you decide? With duct tape, of course.

And how will you learn to apply this *Educational Duct Tape*? With some stories! I hope you'll enjoy them.

Participate in the Adjacent Possible and share your takeaways
with other Duct Tapers: EduDuctTape.com/hub/chapter01

TWO

PJ PANTS, TATER TOTS, AND DOCTORS' OFFICES

Now it's time for me to talk to you about duct tape . . .

and educational technology . . .

and how, in my goofy mind, the two things can go together to form an educational technology integration mindset.

To understand how to use the Educational Duct Tape EdTech Integration Mindset, you need to understand where it comes from. And to understand where it comes from, it's probably best to talk about how I earned the opportunity to write a book like this.

Let's time travel back to March 2019. My wife and kids were in line for a cup of butterbeer in The Wizarding World of Harry Potter at Universal Orlando. While they waited to overpay for a themed, sugary drink, I sat down for a rest outside of Weasley's Wizard Wheezes, pulled out my phone, and opened up Instagram. Seeing hundreds of new followers shocked me. *Something's wrong with Instagram*, I thought. *This can't be right. I haven't posted anything in weeks.* But it was right. Confused, yet pleased, I decided to hop on to my preferred social media platform, Twitter, where I saw a spike in my number of followers. What was going on!? After some inves-

tigation, I discovered that the cause of this jump was a year-old #EduGIF I had shared on Twitter the week before. Without me knowing it, some other people, mostly from other countries, had shared it on Twitter and Instagram. One of those Tweets, from someone in Malaysia, currently has over 81,000 Retweets and 150,000 likes. I wasn't even the one who Tweeted it. It was the most popular Tweet of the #EduGIF, but it wasn't the only one. Other tweets had thousands of interactions as well. The #EduGIF even ended up on Reddit, where, as of this writing, it

> **You're probably wondering, "What is an #EduGIF?"** To see the one that created all of the hubbub on that March day, head to this link (jakemiller.net/translate). That particular #EduGIF was just one of more than 100 #EduGIFs I've created over the past few years. I share them on my website and on social media. Many educators (and even non-educators!) love them for the way they provide quick, clear instruction on how to use a technological tool.

has nearly 90,000 upvotes. The irony, though, is I wasn't even aware what was happening until most of those shares, Retweets, likes, and upvotes had already happened.

I'm not sharing about this #EduGIF going viral to brag, partially because this would be a weird thing to brag about ("Hey, my #EduGIF is super popular in Malaysia!"), but also because this isn't the focus of the book. The focus of this book is helping you make educational technology decisions for your classroom. And this story will help me get there. So let's talk about where these #EduGIFs came from. And, of course, how this can apply to you and your classroom.

What's a GIF? A GIF, which stands for Graphics Interchange Format, is a file type that has been around since the dawn of the internet. Typically, GIFs are a few seconds of video without audio that play in a loop. Most often, they are excerpts from movies, television shows, or sporting events. They are typically small files, so they're easy to send in text messages or Tweets.

What's an #EduGIF? Continue reading to find out!

It all started a little more than fifteen years ago, when I started a new job as a middle school math teacher. I thought it was the best job ever. I loved the district. I loved the school. I loved the content. I loved my students. I could easily imagine staying in that exact role for more than three decades until retirement—nothing sounded better to me at the time. During the next few years, however, I kept being inspired to try new things. I went from teaching eighth-grade math to teaching fourth-grade math to eighth-grade science, to co-writing the curriculum for and teaching a middle school STEM (science, technology, engineering, and math) course. Through all of those iterations of myself as an educator, I discovered my true passion: educational technology.

With each new classroom venture, I became more excited about what technology could do for learning. At first, I implemented edtech to improve my direct instruction. Over time, I had my students use technology because I was excited about what it could do for their learning experiences. Then I started sharing these strategies and tools with my teaching team and, later, my colleagues across my school building and the entire district. A point came where even that wasn't enough; I wanted to share with educators from around the world to indirectly benefit all of their students.

I didn't realize it at the time, but I was experiencing one of my earliest applications of educational duct tape. I had a goal—sharing educational technology with more educators to indirectly benefit more students—and I identified tools that would help me solve that goal:

- *Camtasia*, for video editing and screen recording
- *YouTube*, for hosting the videos
- *A WordPress Site*, for cataloging all of the videos in one place
- *Twitter*, for sharing the videos

In the evening, after my wife and I had convinced our three kids to go to sleep, packed all of the lunches for the next day, and cleaned the kitchen, I would head downstairs to my office (*Which, really, is just a desk with a power strip in the corner of the room where my kids build with LEGO bricks*). I would wear my dress shirt from that day along with my pajama pants (*because you can't see my pajama pants in the video!*). With my beer just off-camera (*Hey, it's late and I'm working hard; don't judge me!*), I would record a screencast about whatever tech tool I was excited to share with educators. Maybe it was Google Classroom, maybe it was Scratch, maybe Google Drawings. Between planning, recording, re-recording, editing, and posting, each video took me between one and two hours to create. But I thought, *If a few dozen educators watch this video, it could benefit thousands of students. That's worth my time.*

I would then upload the video to YouTube, post it on my website, and share it on Twitter. Avoiding checking the number of views and retweets was about as easy as avoiding scratching a mosquito bite. But I could usually resist the urge to check the view count for about a week. When I finally looked, I often discovered seven views. Eight views. Nine, if I was lucky. The truly depressing part is that two of those views were **me** making sure the video was working and one was my mom, a retired teacher who doesn't need to worry about educational technology anymore. So that left me with four views.

What was wrong with my video? Why was that happening?

My video was good. My content was relevant. The production was above average. I was confident it would bring value to educators. It wasn't like a bunch of educators were watching it and saying it wasn't good. They just weren't watching.

But why not?

After observing my own behaviors when discovering educational technology videos and content that other educators shared online or on social media, I realized that I had too many hurdles in place. Educators had to . . .

- have a Twitter account
- follow me
- trust me enough to click on the YouTube link I had posted
- have enough of that trust to believe it was going to be worth the six or seven minutes it would take to watch the video
- have six or seven minutes to spare
- plug in their headphones or be in a place where they could listen to a video

With all those obstacles, much of my potential audience scrolled on or clicked away.

What was I to do? How could I reduce the size and number of the hurdles so that educators would watch my videos and, more importantly, benefit from the educational technology ideas they featured?

The answer came to me in a doctor's office waiting room. I had just filled out my paperwork for my appointment (even though my address, emergency contacts, and insurance information had been the same for the past ten years' worth of appointments). I sat down, and while waiting for the nurse to call me back, scrolled through Facebook. I liked filling these minutes of downtime by seeing what kinds of fun things my friends and family were up to. And then it happened.

Tater tot casserole. *Tater tot casserole* happened.

There, on my Facebook feed, was a video about how to make tater tot casserole. I'm not sure why I watched it, but I watched the whole darn thing. I watched from the browning of the meat all the way through to the serving of the dish. And get this: I do very little of the cooking at our house. My wife, who does the majority of our cooking, already makes tater tot casserole. It's delicious. We don't need a new recipe. We don't need a video about how to make it. Plus, in this video, they put frozen peas into the tater tot casserole. Yuck.

> **Want to watch it for yourself?**
> eduducttape.com/tatertotcasserole

When it was over, I had questions. Who would put peas in a tater tot casserole? More importantly, why did I watch this entire video? Why didn't I scroll right past it like I did with memes riddled with grammatical errors and Buzzfeed personality quizzes? What made this video different?

- **The video auto-played**. As soon as I scrolled to that point in my Facebook feed, the video started playing.
- **It wasn't that long**. I only had to watch for a minute or two.
- **It didn't require any audio**. No headphones necessary. No need to disrupt the people around me with sound. I could understand the video without any audio.

And finally, the video was well made.

It got my attention and presented no hurdles for me to jump over. And finally, it kept my attention with its quality.

That's what my content needs, I thought. Fewer hurdles. Autoplay. No decisions about whether to press play. No headphones. No sound. Quality. Quick.

At the time, I was using Camtasia to create my videos. I was aware Camtasia could also export videos as GIFs, but I had never done it. I had never needed to, but now it seemed like maybe I *did* need to. (By the way, GIF starts with a hard G like gift, not soft G, like giraffe. We can still be friends if you pronounce with the soft G, but we will be better friends if you pronounce it with a hard G.)

Anyhow, I tried it out. The next night, after my wife and I had put the kids in bed, packed the lunches, and made the kitchen sparkle, I headed downstairs to my kids' LEGO roo . . . *er*, my office. But this time, I didn't need the dress shirt. Because I wouldn't have the webcam on. I didn't even need a microphone. And I didn't need to hide my beer. I just needed to make a GIF. What I first discovered was that making a thirty-second GIF took me about as long as making a 7-minute video. As Mark Twain is credited as saying, "I would have written a shorter letter, but I didn't have time." It turns out, being clear and concise takes a lot of work!

The more important discovery, however, came after I completed that first GIF. Instead of seven views in the first week, I probably had seven views in the first hour. And it grew from there. People loved the #EduGIF idea. I had removed many of the hurdles—the #EduGIFs autoplayed, without audio, and were concise—and, as I had suspected, my content was valuable to educators, and they were excited enough about the quality to watch the GIF.

> **See the EduGIF here:** eduducttape.com/firstedugif
> **and the video here:** eduducttape.com/resizingvideo

As I reflected on this experience, I had a big realization. You see, it wasn't my goal to create an #EduGIF or even a regular GIF. Also, before the tater tot casserole happened, it wasn't my goal to create a video either. My goal was to support educators in their use of educational technology so they could support, inspire, and teach students. And with that realization, a belief about technology started to take shape. No duct tape yet, but a belief nonetheless: Technology is most useful when used to solve a problem or meet a goal.

Technology is most useful when used to solve a problem or meet a goal.

Online Resource Hubs

Each chapter in this book features an *#EduDuctTape Question.* These questions will be a question you, as an educator, may ask. I will then provide you a handful of technology tools that could answer that question.

As I told you back in Chapter 1, if I dedicate all of the pages in this book to telling you about the best educational technology tools available to you and your students, it'll be outdated before the ink dries. So, each of these sections will feature a special *Online Resource Hub.* At that link, you will find the following:

- Video tutorials from me
- Curated video tutorials from educators I trust
- Expanded information about the tools discussed in the chapter
- Updates to the information provided
- Additional tools
- A space for you to discuss the chapter and the tools with other readers

Check out this chapter's Online Resource Hub at EduDuctTape.com/hub/chapter02.

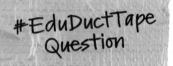

#EduDuctTape Question

How can I create bite-sized instructions for how to do something with technology?

Online Resource Hub—EduDuctTape.com/hub/chapter02

Decide: Is this #EduDuctTape question (above) one I need the answer to?

☐ **YES!** Continue below.   ☐ **NO!** Skim, if you'd like, then move on to the next chapter.

Go ahead, check one. You paid for this book.

That librarian you feared in your childhood can't stop you now.

▶ **THINK:** If your answer was *yes,* ask yourself, "What would it look like if I found the tool that answered the question?" Try to identify some characteristics of what the ideal tool— and its effects—would look like in your classroom.

What would a bite-sized instructions-making tool that's perfect **for me, my classroom, my students,** and **my content** look like? What does it need to do?

_____

_____

_____

_____

_____

_____

_____

▶ **TRY IT OUT!** At the end of this section, I'm going to ask you, "Which tool are you going to try out?" I'm also going to ask you to prioritize trying it out and identify when you'll do so!

TOOLS FOR CREATING #EDUGIFS

The obvious answer here is what we just talked about—#EduGIFs—but it's important to point out that, for many readers of this book, there may not be a need for you to make any #EduGIFs. And that's okay!

You might be a tech coach, tech teacher, or that teacher who voluntarily shares tech tips with everyone. If so, this section is for you. Or maybe you introduce so many new technological tools or processes in your class that you need to provide instructions on using them. If so, this section may also be for you.

If, however, you rarely (or never) need to provide any instructions about using tech tools, this section may _not_ be for you. And, again, that's okay!

That's how these _This Chapter's #EduDuctTape Question_ sections will go. You may or may not have the question or goal that the section covers. That will leave you with a choice to make. You can read it to see whether you can gain anything from the ideas covered or move on to the next chapter. It's your choice!

Now, back to the question. There are two answers I'd like to cover here, and the first is #EduGIFs.

> ### "Whoa, that's a lot of options!"
>
> I'm going to share a bunch of options in many of these tools sections. You don't need to learn them all. You should _not_ try to use them all. You've got some decisions to make! Grab a pencil, so I can guide you through the process.

Camtasia

Educators have asked me on Twitter how I make my #EduGIFs so many times I've created an autotext shortcut on my phone. If I type *usecamtasia*, my phone will insert "I use @Camtasia. If I was on some weird, deserted island that has Wi-Fi, my two required pieces of software would be @GoogleChrome and Camtasia."

Camtasia is a screen-recording and video-editing program that works on Apple and Windows computers. Camtasia is the top-of-the-line video creation tool from the Techsmith company. Users typically employ Camtasia to create videos that involve screen recording, but it is useful for video editing as well.

If you were creating a YouTube channel or a robust online course involving screencasting, Camtasia would be an ideal tool choice. For most classroom screen recording purposes, though, there are less expensive products that you can get by with. We will discuss them later in the book.

If you intend to use the tool to create animated #EduGIFs like mine, Camtasia really is the best option out there. Below are some features and capabilities that set Camtasia apart:

- ✓ *Modifying Speed*—To make a clear and concise #EduGIF, it's essential that you can make some parts go faster and others go slower.
- ✓ *Freeze Frame*—Want to make sure the viewer saw the content in that dropdown menu? Freeze that frame for an extra second or two.
- ✓ *Cursor Effects*—Help the viewer follow along by showing them where and when you're clicking!
- ✓ *Editing Tools*—It's almost impossible to make your #EduGIF concise if you can't cut out parts of the recording!
- ✓ *Annotations*—Since you can't use your voice in an #EduGIF, you'll need textboxes, arrows, circles, and more to communicate information to the viewer.
- ✓ *Blurring*—Keeping student information or your own personal information private is important.
- ✓ *Pan and Zoom*—The *Custom Animation* tool helps focus the viewer's attention on certain areas.
- ✓ *Output Quality*—With Camtasia, you can make sure your GIF files are neither too large nor too low quality. Twitter, for example, limits GIFs to 15 megabytes (mb), and some social media management tools limit them to 5 mb. For general use, you'll want your files to be small enough to load easily but large enough to look good.

Other #EduGIF Creation Tools

Okay, so you learned about Camtasia and you might be thinking one of two things:

1. "You realize I'm on a teacher's salary right, Jake!? That's an expensive piece of software!"
2. "That seems really complex, Jake! Is there something that's a bit simpler?"

Well, I think that you're right to ask both of those questions, dear reader. Camtasia is pricey and feature-rich, but it's worth it if you want to use it extensively to make GIFs or screencasts.

What if you just want to use something that's less expensive and less complicated? You're going to have to compromise your quality, but that might be okay in many situations. Here are some alternatives:

	WeVideo	If you've got a paid education account with WeVideo, you can create GIFs with almost all of the features I listed above.
	Screencastify	The free version of Screencastify lets you export your videos as GIFs. You'll be able to do tons of editing in its free editor including trimming off the beginning or end of your recording, adding cursor effects, using annotation tools, adding emojis, cutting parts out of the recording, adding customizable text, zooming in, cropping out parts of the recordings, and blurring over sensitive or distracting information in your recording. As you can tell, this is pretty close to what I do in Camtasia!
	Screencast-O-Matic	Edit your videos and export them as GIFs in the paid version!
	ScreenToGif.com	This is a great, free tool for Windows PC users! It has an extensive set of editing features too!
	GIFit!	If none of the options above work for you, try this hack: upload a screencast made in another tool to YouTube, then use the GIFit! Chrome Extension to convert part of the screencast into a GIF.
	Snagit	Snagit is an awesome screenshot tool from TechSmith that can also make GIFs, albeit with very limited editing options.

A more extensive table is available at the Online Resource Hub!

iorad

If your goal is bite-sized technology instructions, but you don't want to create an #EduGIF, your best alternative would be iorad.

If you give your students a new tech tool, they're going to ask for step-by-step instructions. And if you give them step-by-step instructions, they're going to ask for screenshots. And if you give them screenshots, they're going to ask you to annotate them. It sounds like an *If You Give a Mouse a Cookie* book, right? Creating these types of tutorials can be tedious and time-consuming.

Iorad automates this process. This Chrome extension or Mac/Windows software tool creates a step-by-step guide, complete with screenshots, for you while you run through the steps that you'd like your students to follow. Once your capture is complete, iorad will show you the step-by-step guide, which you can modify and edit to get it just right.

Your students can access these instructions as a silent video, a PDF, or an interactive tutorial that they click through. This flexibility is one of my favorite parts of this tool: not only does it save you time in the creation of the tutorial, but students can choose to view the tutorial in the format that works best for them.

DECISION TIME!

Are you going to try out one of these tools? ☐ Yes ☐ No

Which one(s)?

- ☐ Camtasia
- ☐ WeVideo
- ☐ Screencastify
- ☐ Screencast-O-Matic
- ☐ ScreenToGif.com

- ☐ GIFit!
- ☐ Snagit
- ☐ Iorad
- ☐ Something else:_____

When are you going to try it out?

☐ Do Now   ☐ Do Soon   ☐ Do Later

Is there a certain lesson, activity, topic, or unit you'll use it for?

_____

_____

If it might solve a problem or meet one of your goals, it's worth committing to trying it out!

Don't forget to check out the resources and tutorials at the Online Resource Hub! There's probably a video about using the tool that you've selected!

EduDuctTape.com/hub/chapter02

THREE

BOUNCE HOUSES, ROLLING PINS, AND DUCT TAPE

From my experience with tater tot casserole, I had learned to look at technology as a tool I could use to solve a problem or meet a goal. Now where did the duct tape come from? To answer that question, I'll need to tell you another story.

THE BOUNCE HOUSE

But first, let me give you a little insight on my wife, April. First of all, she is wonderful, kind, intelligent, and beautiful (*Hi, Honey!*). But the most important thing to understand about her is that she segments the year into three seasons:

- Preparing for our kids' birthday parties
- Planning our kids' Halloween costumes
- Purchasing our kids' Christmas presents

Literally on October 31, she starts Christmas shopping. During each season, parties, costumes, and presents dominate our conversations while we go through our evening ritual of packing lunches and cleaning the kitchen.

Well, this particular story falls during the buying Christmas presents season. It was one of those evenings after the kids were in bed and we were well into our evening work. While I cleaned smooshed green beans off the high chair tray, April showed me a picture on her phone of an eight-foot-diameter inflatable indoor bounce house. I gasped.

No, please, no, I thought. I knew what season it was. I knew what was happening.

And then she said, as I feared, "I think we should get this for the kids for Christmas."

I responded, "What!? Are you crazy!? That thing has an eight-foot diameter! It will take up our entire living room. We already have no room to walk without stepping on toys. Where are we going to put this thing!? Why would you want to do that?"

"Because it will make the kids happy."

Ugh. She had me there. I do love seeing them happy. And she was right; I knew that the bounce house would make them as happy as teachers on bagels-in-the-staff-lounge day. It probably wouldn't have mattered whether I agreed to it or not, but I agreed. She purchased it on the spot.

The man in the red suit delivered the bounce house on December 24, but that lazy guy did not inflate it. Who inflated it? Me, of course. And so began my love–hate relationship with the bounce house.

I *loved* how happy it made my kids, because—believe me—on December 25,

Here's the bounce house in our old living room.

they were so excited to play in it. But I *hated* how much work I had to put into it. Because on the twenty-seventh, when they were already tired of it and it was in their way too, I was the guy who had to deflate it. I was the guy who opened up all the valves and rolled around on top of it like a six-foot-four-inch rolling pin to push all the air out. After a dozen rolls back and forth, I was the guy who folded it up and put it in our basement.

Once every month or two, I would get it back out and re-inflate it for the kids to play in. Each time, they had a blast with it. Each time, a day or two later they were over it once again. And then it was my time. Time for me to transform into the human rolling pin. Back and forth, back and forth until all the air was out and I could fold it up.

This inflate, play, deflate, roll, fold, inflate, play, deflate, roll, fold cycle lasted for years. Until one day when I was inflating the bounce house for the kids, I heard a faint *fsssss* sound. And when the bounce house made this sound, I went into Mr. Burns mode. Do you know Mr. Burns from *The Simpsons*? Can you picture him maniacally whispering "Yes. Excellent," while tapping his fingers together? Well, that was me. I was so excited that I could finally throw out the bounce house!

But then I noticed that my kids were giggling at the *fsssss* sound. When I saw them, I smiled at how adorable they were and realized that, regardless of how glorious it would feel to throw the thing out, I had to patch it. After all, it made them happy. That was always the goal! And they were so cute when they were happy. So I had to fix it for them. How would I patch an inflatable bounce house?

Go ahead and take a guess.

I had a problem, and I needed to select a tool to help me solve that problem. A tool that was readily available, relatively easy to use, and solved the problem. And what tool was it?

Duct tape.

Of course it was duct tape! And the duct tape worked phenomenally. It was easy to apply, and it successfully kept the hole patched and the bounce house inflated.

So, how did this experience with an indoor bounce house lead to the creation of an educational technology integration mindset? Well, that part came later.

THE THREE TYPES OF PEOPLE AT AN EDTECH CONFERENCE

A few months down the road, at an educational technology conference, I sat sipping my coffee and observing the educators as they took part in a day of learning. I noticed that you could pretty easily fit the attendees into one of three profiles.

- *Michael*—"Wow! Flipgrid is so cool! I'm going to use it in my class tomorrow!"
  Pam—"Great! What are you teaching tomorrow?"
  Michael—"I don't know, but I'm going to use Flipgrid!"

We love Michael's enthusiasm for trying new technology in his classroom, but it's concerning that Michael selects the tool without any regard for what he's trying to achieve in his classroom.

- *Phyllis*—"Oh jeez, there are too many technology tools to learn. How will I ever learn them all!? I am so overwhelmed."

We can certainly understand where Phyllis is coming from on this. There are lots of tech tools. And if you tried to learn all of them, it would be insanely overwhelming. But do we have to learn all of them?

- *Jim*—"Wow, look at all of these cool tech tools. Flipgrid looks like it'll be great when I want to hear each student's voice. Pear Deck looks like it will be nice when I'd like to lead a direct instruction lesson and formatively assess my learners as I go. Google Drawings looks like a great way for students to visually represent their thinking. Scratch looks like a great tool for kids to design interactive animations and games. I will put all of these tools into my educational technology toolbox, and I will pull them out when they fit my goals or learning standards for a given lesson."

While we love Michael's enthusiasm and we can empathize with Phyllis's stress, it's clear that Jim has the right perspective. The educational technology tools are just that: tools. We can place

Educational technology is at its most useful when it is not the goal of the lesson, but a tool used to solve a problem, meet a goal, or address a learning standard.

them into our toolbox today and worry about learning to use them when we need them.

I didn't wake up that day planning to use duct tape. The duct tape didn't come up until I had a problem that needed solving. Back in Chapter 2, I wasn't planning to create GIFs or even to use Camtasia. I used Camtasia to make GIFs when I had a goal those GIFs could address.

And from there, these three disconnected stories—the tater tot casserole, the bounce house, and the educational technology conference—merged into one edtech integration mindset:

Educational technology is at its most useful when it is not the goal of the lesson, but a tool used to solve a problem, meet a goal, or address a learning standard.

Similarly, using duct tape is never one's goal, but it is an incredibly useful tool when solving problems or helping you meet a goal.

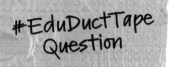

#EduDuctTape Question

How can I formatively assess my students' comprehension?

Online Resource Hub—EduDuctTape.com/hub/chapter03

As you now know, a key part of the *Educational Duct Tape* mindset is identifying problems, goals, or needs that we have in our practice as educators or in our classrooms. This often means that, as educators, we need some data—quantitative (measured) or qualitative (observed)—that we can reflect on.

We refer to the data used to help us identify problems, goals, or needs as *formative* data. Formative assessment is the means by which we acquire the data that help us identify next steps with regard to how and what to teach our students.

Formative assessment is also called assessment *for* learning. In other words, it is used *for* determining next steps. According to educator and author Dylan William, assessments are formative "if and only if something is contingent on their outcome, and the information is actually used to alter what would have happened in the absence of the information."

A Note from the Author: John Hattie's Effect Sizes

When appropriate, I will reference the work of John Hattie, professor of education and director of the Melbourne Education Research Institute at the University of Melbourne, Australia. Hattie's *Visible Learning* work quantifies the student achievement effects of many possible influences. Although Hattie's work doesn't evaluate the effects of specific technological tools, it does evaluate effects of specific pedagogical strategies and influences. By looking at that information, we can determine how important it is to find a technological tool to assist us in that effort.

Hattie's quantification of student achievement effects come from a "synthesis of many meta-analyses" of educational studies. In other words, he did not do the study or gather the data; rather, he looked at and compared a collection of studies that others completed. His work yields a quantity that he calls an *effect size*.

A zero effect size means the item has no effect on student achievement. Positive effect sizes enhance student achievement and, as you'd guess, negative ones decrease it.

In Hattie's first book on the subject, *Visible Learning*, he wrote that an effect size of 1.0 "is typically associated with advancing children's achievement by two to three years, [or] improving the rate of learning by 50 percent." He continues, "When implementing a new program, an effect size of 1.0 would mean that, on average, students receiving that treatment would exceed 84 percent of students not receiving that treatment." To put these effect sizes into perspective, in his most recent list, the highest was 1.57 and the lowest was –0.90.

Most people would conclude that an influence that has a higher effect size (let's say, 1.2) is automatically more valuable to implement than one with a lower effect size (let's say, 0.95), Hattie points out that it's not that cut and dried. The 1.2 effect size influence, for example, may be costly and intensive to implement, while the 0.95 effect size influence may be inexpensive and easy to implement. Obviously, there are always other factors at play.

Because there are a variety of factors to consider, a good number to keep in mind is 0.40. Hattie calls this number "the hinge-point." This is "where effects of innovation enhance achievement in such a way that we can notice real-world differences." Although some innovations falling between 0.0 and 0.40 are worthy of consideration, Hattie calls those that are above 0.40 the "zone of desired effects."

In his more recent work, he breaks the items into five tiers:

- **0.70 and above**—Potential to considerably accelerate student achievement
- **0.40–0.70**—Potential to accelerate student achievement
- **0.20–0.40**—Likely to have positive impact on student achievement
- **0.0–0.20**—Likely to have small positive impact on student achievement
- **Below 0**—Likely to have a negative impact on student achievement

Robert E. Stake famously said, "When the cook tastes the soup, that's formative; when the guests taste the soup, that's summative." In his earliest meta-synthesis, Hattie identified "providing formative evaluation" as one of the highest-ranking influences for student learning. In his more recent studies, the data show the influence being slightly lower, though still impactful. In his 2018 meta-synthesis, he has found it to have a 0.48 effect size, placing it within the zone of desired effects and the *potential to accelerate student achievement* tier.

Although most activities or tools can yield qualitative or quantitative data that you can use formatively, some tools are built specifically for obtaining formative assessment data and doing so efficiently. We'll revisit this topic across a few different chapters, but in this one we'll focus on some easy-to-implement tools that provide access to lots of data that we can use to determine next steps.

> **Decide:** Is this #EduDuctTape question (How can I formatively assess my students' comprehension?) one I need the answer to?
>
> ☐ **YES!** Continue below.   ☐ **NO!** Skim, if you'd like, then move on to the next chapter.

▶ **Think:** What would a formative assessment tool that's perfect **for me, my classroom, my students,** and **my content** look like? What does it need to do?

_____

_____

_____

_____

_____

FORMATIVE ASSESSMENT TOOLS FOR QUICK INSIGHTS

Quizizz

This tool uses points, power-ups, memes, and competition to make formative assessment fun for your students, while giving you some great data. Check it out:

✓ You can add multiple choice, checkbox (multiple correct answers), fill-in-the-blank, poll, and open-ended questions.

✓ You can host synchronous whole-class Quizizz games.

✓ Your students compete as individuals or in randomly grouped, anonymous teams.

✓ You can see progress and rankings as the game takes place.

✓ Your students progress through questions at their own rate.

✓ You can choose whether you'd like to reward your students for speed.

✓ You can set up asynchronous games or practice sessions.

✓ You can assign your sets as homework.

✓ Your students can use sets as flash cards.

As the aforementioned "When the cook tastes the soup, that's formative . . ." quotation indicates, if a tool is to be useful for formative assessment, it must provide some sort of data that can guide your decisions. In other words, our data—the taste test—need to tell us whether the soup is ready to go to the restaurant guests or needs additional ingredients first. Quizizz provides those data by showing you detailed data summaries organized by student as well as by question.

Later in the book, I'll share about Quizizz Lessons, which can combine its formative assessment capabilities with lesson delivery features.

Quizlet

Quizlet has been the go-to online flashcard tool for years. Teachers love its ease of use, and students love that they can practice at any time and in a variety of ways aside from the default flashcards mode.

When Quizlet rolled out Quizlet Live a few years ago, teachers and students flipped for it. This live game randomly groups classmates to try to answer all of the questions from a flashcard set. The fun part of the game is that each student sees a different set of possible answers to the questions that his or her team is trying to answer. So, although they all see the same question, the correct answer is on only one of their screens.

The problem with Quizlet Live as a formative assessment tool is that you do not get much useful data from any of this, aside from a screen that shows terms that your students learned during the session and which ones they should study more or already knew.

Kahoot

If you've never heard of Kahoot, you may just have been living under a rock in 2015. I hope that doesn't offend you but, seriously, it was *all the rage* in classrooms and professional developments at around that time. And with good reason! It offered a fun way for students to review information and for teachers to get some formative assessment data. Why am I using the past tense here? I'm not sure! It's still a useful tool. It's no longer *all the rage*, but that doesn't mean you shouldn't consider using it! Here's what it lets you and your students do:

- ✓ Project a quiz (multiple choice) or true/false question on the board.
- ✓ Your students attempt to click the appropriate choice (they're color-coded and have different shapes on them) on their own screens before time is up.
- ✓ You can enable the option to display the questions and answers on your students' devices.
- ✓ Your students earn points for correct answers (with a bonus for answering faster).
- ✓ Your students see the rankings for the top performers on your screen.
- ✓ Your students play games in teams or as individuals. You have the option to have the game pause between questions for a powerful review-or-reteach opportunity.
- ✓ Assign Kahoots for asynchronous independent work in game mode or in one of the *study* modes (*flashcards*, *practice*, *test yourself*, and *challenge* modes).
- ✓ You can access a bank of questions from other Kahoot users.

The pro and premium versions offer a few additional elements:

- ★ Personalized learning paths that bring back previously missed questions
- ★ Additional question types:
  - ▶ Multi-select answers
  - ▶ Puzzles—drag words, numbers, or letters into the correct order
  - ▶ Polls
  - ▶ In *image reveal* questions, the image is gradually revealed while students attempt to answer the question.
  - ▶ Type answer
- ★ Access to slides to deliver content or instructions
- ★ Collaboration with colleagues

Students love Kahoot for its exhilarating competition, and teachers love it for the data. In the free version of Kahoot, you can see data summaries organized by each question, which helps you identify which ones you need to work on with the class. In the free version, you cannot see which questions individual students got right or wrong.

Gimkit

Kahoot	=	the formative assessment fad of 2015.
Quizlet Live	=	the formative assessment fad of 2017.
Gimkit	=	the formative assessment fad of 2019. It's still great in 2021 and beyond, but you'll probably need the paid version to make it work in your classroom.

Gimkit was developed by Josh Feinsilber as a project in his project-based learning high school. And, just to be clear, he wasn't a teacher there. He was a student. Josh said, "I built Gimkit to be the game I wanted to play in class!" Students' excited reactions to the game prove that Josh succeeded. Check out the features:

- ✓ Ask multiple choice or text input questions.
- ✓ Your students earn (fake) cash for correct answers and streaks of correct answers.
- ✓ Your students can "spend" their cash on power-ups and upgrades.
- ✓ Your students will love special game modes based off of popular trends like *The Avengers* and *Among Us*.
- ✓ See each of your students' performances question-by-question or look at a full class summary after game's end.
- ✓ You can assign kits for asynchronous use.
- ✓ You can import kits from other tools.
- ✓ You can export kits to other tools.
- ✓ You can use KitCollab to have students collaboratively create kits.

In the years since it launched, Gimkit has continually improved. Also, Josh has graduated from high school. Another thing that changed over the years, though, is Gimkit's pricing. Fortunately, it's inexpensive; you can only use kits with five students at a time in the free version.

Quizalize

The basic features of Quizalize are pretty similar to the tools above, but its *Mastery Dashboard* makes it worth adding into this list. Here's what you can do:

- ✓ See standard-by-standard how each student (or your entire class) is performing.
- ✓ Select differentiated next steps (YouTube videos, pdf documents, or a link to anywhere on the web) that will be assigned based on your students' scores.

✓ Choose from Quizalize's curated remedial and enrichment resources.

✓ Use multiple choice, sorting, matching, ordering, and text response questions.

✓ Use videos, audio, images, and math type in your questions.

✓ Require your students to keep going until they get all of the questions right with *Mastery Mode*.

✓ Score bubble-sheet assessments with their scanning app.

✓ Add some fun with team games.

You're probably thinking, "Jake, why did you list this tool fifth!? It sounds awesome-sauce!" Well (*cue the Debbie Downer trombone*) the thing keeping us all from rushing out to adopt this tool is the cost. If you want to use it more than five times in one class, you'll need to pay to upgrade. The cost seems pretty fair, but I know that you were hoping that the cost was *zero dollars and zero cents*. If you want standards-based mastery tracking and automated differentiation, though, it might be worth it.

Blooket

This tool snuck onto my radar shortly before I pressed *Send* on this manuscript. Which is appropriate, because it's packed to the gills with games that deliver excitement for each student right until the last second of the game.

Blooket (pronounced *blue-kit*) often gets described as "like Gimkit or Kahoot," which is partially accurate. That description, however, fails to cover just how many ways Blooket will make most of your students cheer, laugh, and yell while gamifying review, formative assessment, and vocabulary learning.

✓ Questions are all multiple choice.

✓ Questions can be either text or images.

✓ Games can be played live or asynchronously.

✓ Questions can be imported from Quizlet or a spreadsheet.

✓ Your students can create accounts to earn and collect *blooks* (small character icons).

Blooket's main mode of use is for live classroom games. The company adds new games regularly, but here are the live games that are available at the time of this writing:

✓ *Classic* mode is Kahoot-like and gives you opportunities to review answers with the class as you go.

✓ *Racing* mode places your students on a virtual racetrack, using power-ups to jump forward or send classmates backwards.

✓ *Battle Royale* pits your students against their classmates in randomly assigned battles to see who can survive for the longest. There is also a team-based option for Battle Royale.

✓ *Factory* mode puts your students in charge of their own factory, where correct answers allow them to add and upgrade the "workers" in their factory to level up their factory's earnings faster and faster. Your students will enjoy employing strategic moves in this game, and the *glitches*, which they can use to hinder their classmates, add to the fun!

✓ *Tower Defense* uses a similar strategic format, in which your students' correct answers allow them to purchase and upgrade towers that let them earn points by defeating evil *blooks*.

✓ *Café* mode is another strategy-based game. In this one, your students answer questions to earn food to sell to café customers. As the customers purchase food, your students can use that money to upgrade their café's menu to earn more money faster.

✓ *Gold Quest* mode leverages luck to bring the excitement. Correct answers earn your students treasure chests to open that contain surprises that could help them, hurt them, or even let them steal gold from their classmates. This intense gameplay continues until the last second, and even struggling students have a shot at winning.

✓ *Crypto Hack* mode is pretty similar to *Gold Quest* except it replaces treasure chests with the cryptocurrency buzz of 2021. When your students answer questions correctly, they earn opportunities to hack into each other's winnings or assign them tedious tasks to complete.

Some Blooket games can be played asynchronously. Asynchronous games remove the focus on speed but maintain all of the fun, excitement, and gamification.

✓ In *Tower of Doom*, correct answers earn your students battle cards that can be used to defeat villains and make it through the tower of doom.

✓ In *Crazy Kingdom*, your students answer questions to maintain their kingdom's resources, residents, happiness, and gold while dealing with the requests of the *crazy* guests who come to visit.

✓ The *Factory*, *Café*, and *Tower Defense* modes, covered above, can also be played asynchronously.

While tasting the soup (playing Blooket) is fun, does it help the cook (you) improve the final dish (your students' comprehension)? Well, that depends on whether this taste test lets you identify where improvements are needed. After Blooket games, you can see each of your students' percentage of correct answers as well as the class average. In the free version you cannot, however, see question-by-question data in live games. You can see question-by-question data in asynchronous games. This brings us to the main draw to the paid version: *detailed game reports.* Although the paid version offers other features such as early access to games, the data in those reports constitute the main reason you might consider it.

There Are More!?

Although these six tools are great for formative assessment, there are at least a dozen more that we could discuss. Some, like Socrative, Poll Everywhere, Google Forms, Microsoft Forms, Mentimeter, 99 Math, questions in Google Classroom, and EdPuzzle, do similar things. Another tool, Plickers, even works for classrooms that are not 1:1 with technology. You could also use Flippity.net, which we'll discuss more later, to make Jeopardy-style games, board games, and other formative assessment options. Some of the many options even add in a bonus feature here or there. I don't want to overwhelm you with options, but you can learn more about many of these in the Online Resource Hub.

In a later chapter, we'll focus on some formative assessment tools that might be slightly more complex but could yield richer insights into student learning.

DECISION TIME!

Are you going to try out one of these tools?   ☐ Yes   ☐ No

Which one(s)?

☐ Quizizz   ☐ Quizalize
☐ Quizlet   ☐ Blooket
☐ Kahoot   ☐ Something else:_____
☐ Gimkit

When are you going to try it out?

☐ Do Now   ☐ Do Soon   ☐ Do Later

Is there a certain lesson, activity, topic, or unit you'll use it for?

_____

_____

If it might solve a problem or meet one of your goals, it's worth committing to trying it out!

Don't forget to check out the resources and tutorials at the Online Resource Hub! There's probably a video about using the tool that you've selected!

(EduDuctTape.com/hub/chapter03)

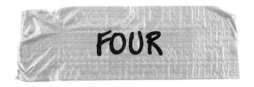

FOUR

WORDS, RESTAURANTS, AND JAMS

They are the stuff of nightmares. No, I'm not talking about zombies or demogorgons. I'm talking about my least favorite six words. And they are words that, when spoken by a significant other, frustrate nearly every adult.

What restaurant should we go to?

Uggghhhhhhh. Those words! They seem so innocent! They actually seem great when you are naive about love and relationships. "I get to pick the restaurant!? This is awesome!" Yet, we soon learn to be wary of these words. Why? Well, it's partially because our partner is rarely in the mood for the restaurant we select first. But there are two even bigger reasons for the stress that comes from these six words:

1. TOO MANY CHOICES

There are so many options to choose from! For most people in America, there are dozens of dinner options within a half-hour drive of our homes. How can you pick just one?

2. TOO MUCH PRESSURE

What if I get it wrong? It feels like it's my fault.

What if the service is bad? It feels like it's my fault.

What if my wife's food is bad? It's my fault.

What if it takes too long and our kids get restless? My fault.

The pressure of selecting the perfect restaurant is not unlike the stress educators feel when selecting new integrations of tech tools for their classrooms. With so many tools to choose from, teachers feel immense pressure to select the right one. Losing a day's lesson to a tech flop can feel downright traumatic. *Sure, it's nice that there are lots of technologies to choose from, but what if I choose incorrectly?*

Oftentimes, the end result with our dinner choices (we give up and let the kids pick) is similar to the end result with our tech tool choices (we give up and don't select any). This, unfortunately, happens more often than not. Ask a group of teachers who attended an educational technology conference, "Have you used any new technologies in your classroom that you learned about at that conference?" I predict that the answers will be depressing. You may have a few positive responses, but you'll have an overwhelming majority of negative ones. Why?

It's the paradox of choice. Psychologist Barry Schwartz eloquently covered this paradox in his TED Talk (and book) *The Paradox of Choice*. In it, he says:

> "All of this choice . . . produces paralysis, rather than liberation. With so many options to choose from, people find it very difficult to choose at all."

This is the exact phenomenon I experience when my wife asks me to select our dinner destination: I'm paralyzed by all of the options, not liberated by them.

It's also the phenomenon that many educators experience when selecting a new technology to learn or use: They feel paralyzed by all of the options, not liberated by them.

In another publication, Schwartz shared about a study done by psychologists Sheena Iyengar and Mark Lepper. In the study, they set up a jam-sampling stand at a grocery store. In some instances, they had twenty-four varieties of jam available for sampling. In other instances, they had only six varieties. While more varieties led to more visitors at the table, *fewer varieties led to more purchases*. People who visited the table when there were only six varieties were ten times more likely to purchase a jam than those who visited when there were twenty-four varieties! Why? The paradox of choice. Having twenty-four options of jam paralyzed the visitors, and so, they opted for none.

Whether it is dinner or jam or the technology for our schools and classrooms, we fear making the wrong choice. In an article in the *Harvard Business Review,* Schwartz said, "Increased choice decreases satisfaction with matters as trivial as ice cream flavors and as significant as jobs." He explains, "it [increased choice] requires increased time and effort and can lead to anxiety, regret, excessively high expectations, and self-blame if the choices don't work out."

The tech tools we use in the classroom probably fall somewhere between ice cream flavors and job choices. Which raises the question, how do we avoid this fear? How do we avoid the paradox of choice? How do we avoid the paralysis caused by having too many options?

We narrow down our choices. That's my strategy for crushing this paradox. Take Iyengar and Lepper's jam-sampling stand, for example. If there are only one or two jams, they may not have one that we like. If there are twenty-four jams, their data show that increased choice will lead to us being unlikely to make a purchase. But if there are six? Then we're more likely to make a choice, less likely to feel anxious or regretful about it, and more likely to be satisfied with our choice than if there were one, two, or twenty-four options.

If my grocery store offers six jam options—grape, strawberry, blackberry, raspberry, apricot, and blueberry—it's going to be relatively easy to choose and be satisfied with the choice. But if there are two versions of each of those six, plus twelve other options (twenty-four total), I might just walk away empty-handed. Unless I narrow it down. If I can narrow it down to some key parameters (a favorite fruit, organic, low sugar, etc.), I stand the chance of having a much easier choice.

If I ask my wife questions about our dinner destination (*Are you in the mood for Mexican food? Would you like to have a drink with dinner? Do you want it to be a fast restaurant or a slower sit-down restaurant?*) I am bound to end up with only a few similar options to choose between. My likelihood of choosing one and feeling good about it will increase.

The same strategy applies to technology integration. If I can narrow down the expansive set of technology tools to just the ones that are good for formative assessment, vocabulary learning, video creation, or whatever I'm seeking to accomplish, then my list of options will be comfortably short. The decision gets a whole lot easier.

The best way to narrow down the list of options for technology integration? It's on the cover of this book.

Educational Technology is most useful when it is not the goal of the lesson but a tool used to solve a problem, meet a goal, or address a learning standard.

If you start by identifying that problem, goal, need, or learning standard, then you have already narrowed your choices down.

How can I get rich formative assessment data about my students' learning?

Online Resource Hub—EduDuctTape.com/hub/chapter04

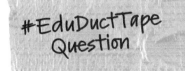
#EduDuctTape Question

FORMATIVE ASSESSMENT TOOLS FOR RICH DATA

In the previous chapter, we explored a set of formative assessment tools that provide formative assessment data quickly and easily. Although those tools are useful and efficient (and often fun for students), we may want to gain a deeper understanding of our students' learning. For that, we'll need tools that ask more than just multiple-choice questions. After all, with multiple-choice questions, it can be hard to differentiate between correct guesses and true comprehension or between partial comprehension and an absence of knowledge. Let's look at some formative assessment tools that can deliver us richer data.

> **Decide:** Is this #EduDuctTape question (above) one I need the answer to?
>
> ☐ **YES!** Continue below.
> ☐ **NO!** Skim, if you'd like, then move on to the next chapter.

▶ **Think:** What would a formative assessment tool that's perfect **for me, my classroom, my students,** and **my content** look like? What does it need to do?

_____

_____

_____

_____

Formative

Could I really make a list of formative assessment tools and exclude a tool named *Formative* (goformative.com)? No. And its name isn't the only reason it gets included. You can use Formative to "see student work in real time, give feedback, track student progress to learning standards, and collaborate around common assessment data." You can:

✓ Ask multiple-choice, multiple selection, true/false, short answer, and essay questions.

✓ Use the *Show Your Work* option to have your students draw, type, or upload an image.

✓ Include images, math type, videos, and embedded internet content in your questions.

✓ Upload existing content—PDFs, images, Google Docs, Google Slides, PowerPoints, and more—and add questions right into them.

Premium accounts add in even more features:

★ You can add audio to questions.

★ Your students can respond with audio.

★ You can two-way message with individual students during the Formative.

★ You can use additional question types (categorize, graphing, matching, numeric, resequence).

The true power of Formative, however, is in the data that you get out of it.

✓ See your students' responses live.

✓ Intervene and support your students on the spot.

✓ See question-by-question, student-by-student, or standard-by-standard data after your students complete the assessment.

Imagine knowing which standards each student in your room has or has not mastered! The catch here is that if you have a free plan you can only see the last two weeks' worth of data within the progress tracker, though you can still access older data in a nonaggregated form.

Classkick

Classkick kicks assessment! Get it? Classkick is similar to Formative and better-known tools such as Pear Deck and Nearpod, which we'll discuss in a later chapter. But Classkick has some features that truly set it apart from the others, especially if your students are on touchscreen devices such as iPads or touchscreen Chromebooks.

✓ Format questions to allow your students to respond with text, uploaded images, images taken on their webcam, audio, links, drawings, or a combination of all of these!

✓ Include images that your students can move around the screen as manipulatives for things like drag-and-drop and ordering activities, which is something that you cannot do in Formative, Pear Deck, or Nearpod.

✓ Set your multiple-choice, multiple selection, and true/false questions to be autograded.

✓ Add fill-in-the-blank questions to images.

✓ Include lots of content in your questions, including:

▶ Drawings

▶ Text

▶ Images

▶ PDFs turned into images

- ▶ Audio
- ▶ Links
- ▶ Videos

What sets Classkick apart from the others, though, are the collaboration, support, and feedback opportunities that you and your students can leverage *during* the formative assessment.

- ✓ You can see your students' responses live.
- ✓ You can jump into a student's response to provide support or feedback.
- ✓ Your students can digitally raise their hand if they need help.
- ✓ Your students can anonymously jump in to help classmates who raise their hand. Only you will know who the two students are: they're anonymous to each other.

Although multiple-choice and short-answer questions can be autograded, you can provide feedback on any question in real time or after the activity ends. Your feedback can include stickers, rubric values, text, pen tool annotations, and even saved lines of text. And then, the cherry on top of the sundae: you can see rich data about your students' performance.

And the sprinkles on top of the cherry on top of the sundae? While you're limited to twenty assignments in the free version, it does include all of the above functions! The paid version combines the ability to have unlimited assignments with some other nice features—organizing assessments in folders, curating student portfolios, and more—but all of the essential pieces? Free.

Edulastic

Some educators embrace Edulastic because it resembles standardized tests and features an available collection of released test questions. For me, those are not compelling reasons to select a tech tool. Fortunately, Edulastic has other worthwhile qualities.

- ✓ An extensive bank of standardized assessment-aligned questions, including released test items
- ✓ A crazy amount of question formats, including these:
  - ▶ The basics (multiple-choice, true/false, multiple selection, essay, matching, a variety of fill-in-the-blank types)
  - ▶ A variety of standardized test-like questions, including those with reading passages
  - ▶ Drawing response questions with a variety of tools, including shapes, a protractor, and more

- ► A variety of drag-and-drop formats, including classification, cloze, resequencing, and sorting formats
- ► Diagram or image labeling
- ► Questions with images, videos, or audio
- ✓ A collection of question types that math teachers will love:
  - ► Responding with numerical and algebraic expressions
  - ► Graphing on the coordinate plane
  - ► Shading in square, rectangle, or circle fraction diagrams
  - ► Modifying data representations, including bar graphs, pictographs, and line plots
  - ► Graphing inequalities on number lines
- ✓ Many autograded question types
- ✓ A *Scratch Pad* that gives your students a space to show their work or explain their reasoning using text, drawing, writing, mathematical text or equations, a protractor, a ruler, and more

If the test prep nature of Edulastic and the variety of interactive question types don't sell you on this tool, the data might.

- ✓ You can see data instantly as your students progress through their assessments.
- ✓ You can see rich, standards-aligned data afterward.

Although the free plan has enough features to inform plenty of instructional decisions, the premium plan includes some additional awesome features:

- ★ More extensive data
- ★ Rubric scoring
- ★ Built-in read-aloud feature
- ★ Built-in Desmos calculators
- ★ *SnapScore* for bubble sheets
- ★ Collaboration between teachers
- ★ Anti-cheating options

If you'd like to have large-scale, standards-aligned, student-mastery data across a school or a district, it's a no-brainer: Edulastic is the tool for you.

Flipgrid

What can this Microsoft-owned, completely free platform *not* do!? Although there probably are a few things (I'm still waiting for an edtech tool that will *also* make me a great cup of French press coffee), I'll be mentioning Flipgrid often in this book. That's because it's a multipurpose tool—and one of those purposes is formative assessment!

Your students can do the following:

✓ Respond with video.

✓ Respond with audio only.

✓ Write or draw in the video.

✓ Type in their video.

✓ Add pictures into the video and even annotate them.

✓ Use a whiteboard (or blackboard) screen.

✓ Use *Backdrops* to add images, videos, or PowerPoint presentations behind them without needing a greenscreen.

✓ Use *Backdrops* to blur their background.

✓ Add music to their videos.

✓ Utilize filters and augmented-reality-like surroundings with *Lenses*.

✓ Screen record.

✓ Edit videos.

✓ Combine videos.

✓ Access fun filters and features.

You can do these things:

✓ Provide feedback with video or text comments.

✓ Make those comments public or private.

✓ Catalog and even curate your students' responses in a *Mixtape* to show growth over time.

Although it is one of my favorite educational tools, Flipgrid has two downsides as a formative assessment tool.

The first is time. Even with the ability to speed up videos or watch them from your phone, watching a video from every student could take a boatload of time. I, like many Flipgrid-using teachers, would argue that it can be worth that time. The power of *hearing* and *seeing* your students explain their thinking is so valuable! It's worth finding ways to work it into your practice as a formative assessment tool when you can. And, when you can't, who said you had to formatively assess *everything*? There is plenty of value in students demonstrating comprehension even if you never assess it or even watch it. *Shhhh . . . don't tell my students I don't watch every Flipgrid video they record!*

The second issue is data. Tools like Edulastic and Formative can provide lots of easy-to-read, standards-aligned data and even autograde some questions, but those features just don't fit with the Flipgrid model. There's no way to score or grade students' videos within the platform, aside from leaving comments, and there's obviously not an autograding feature.

So if it takes a long time to watch the videos, you can't grade responses, and there is no data that shows you who is doing well and who is struggling, why would we use Flipgrid for formative assessment? Simple: you can *hear* from each student and easily provide them with feedback.

Wait, that's still not all of them!?

That's right, there are so many tools that do formative assessment that, despite covering it in two chapters, we *still* have not covered all of them. If you're looking for quick, easy, multiple-choice formative assessments that students enjoy and can inform your next steps on the fly, you probably want to select one of the tools from back in Chapter 3. If you're looking for a tool that you can use throughout the year to analyze and track student comprehension and growth while preparing your students for standardized assessments, you're probably going to stick with the tools right here in Chapter 4. While there are more tools that offer a similar level of formative information—GoSoapBox, Slido, Spiral, InsertLearning, EdCite—there are also tools that combine rich formative assessment with other features. We'll cover some of those tools in a later chapter. We'll also visit the idea of self-assessment in an upcoming chapter.

DECISION TIME!

Are you going to try out one of these tools? ☐ Yes ☐ No

Which one(s)?

☐ Formative   ☐ Flipgrid

☐ Classkick   ☐ Something else:_____

☐ Edulastic

When are you going to try it out?

☐ Do Now   ☐ Do Soon   ☐ Do Later

Is there a certain lesson, activity, topic, or unit you'll use it for?

_____

_____

If it might solve a problem or meet one of your goals, it's worth committing to trying it out!

Don't forget to check out the resources and tutorials at the Online Resource Hub! There's probably a video about using the tool that you've selected!

EduDuctTape.com/hub/chapter04

FIVE

SHIRT SLEEVES, TRANSPARENCY MARKERS, AND THE PRETTY PSYCHOLOGIST

Disclaimer: *In this chapter, I'll be sharing about my earliest uses of SMART Boards. Please understand that the goal is not to share about SMART Boards as a new and exciting tech tool (they're fine, but seriously, 2006 called and they want their edtech back!), but to share about them as a case study of sorts for how we view technology in* Educational Duct Tape.

Back in 2005, I had a big crush on the school psychologist at the middle school I taught at. She was intelligent and beautiful, had a good sense of humor, and was fun to chat with. I remember one day urgently walking up to the main office to chat with the principal about an issue with a student. On my way into the office, the school psychologist walked by me, smiled at me, and said, "Hi."

I turned around, awkwardly jumped in front of her, and held the door open for her. It sounds chivalrous, I know, but it really could not have been more awkward. She looked at me with a surprised look and thanked me, to which I responded, "No, thank you!"

What!? I thought. *Why are you thanking her!? What is wrong with you, Jake!?*

Lost in my embarrassment, I forgot what I was there for, turned around, and walked back to my classroom. I looked like the biggest weirdo of all time.

After a few days of self-loathing, I finally worked up the nerve to stop by her office and chat with her. Standing in the doorway, I delivered my opening line, "Hi! How are you doing?"

She looked up from her computer and said, "Hi! Great!" She smiled, but then her expression changed to concern as she said, "Um, what's that on your sleeve?"

I looked down to discover that the right sleeve of my white dress shirt had quite a bit of blood-colored dried liquid on it. *Ugh.* Expo Vis-a-Vis transparency marker!

After I explained that it was marker, and, in fact, not blood, we had a good laugh. After that conversation, I walked away feeling a little embarrassed and motivated. Motivated to resolve this transparency marker issue.

You see, I taught three periods of eighth-grade math, one period of algebra, and one period of advanced algebra. I taught those classes from atop my trusty stool in front of a transparency projector. Each day I sat, facing my class, with the projector in front of me. I worked out math problems, while my work showed up on the screen behind me. My students feverishly jotted down notes.

At the end of each class, I had blue, red, purple, and green transparency marker ink all over my wrist, forearm and, sometimes, shirt sleeve. But this wasn't the worst of my problems.

To prepare for class, in advance, I wrote out on sheets of transparency paper the equations and problems we would go over in class. Each period, I would pull out the appropriate folder of transparencies and teach the class by doing the work on a blank transparency that I laid over those prepared transparencies. Then I would place the original transparencies back in my folder and clean the ones I had written on during the lesson. I had transparency pages everywhere. I also had residue from the markers everywhere. But that still was not the worst of my problems.

The biggest problem? My lessons were not very good.

I needed to find a way to get better—for my students, for my shirt sleeves, and most of all, for the school psychologist.

The summer between my first and second year in that role, my mother, then an elementary school teacher, invited me to attend a professional development workshop about SMART Boards with her. I had never heard of one, but her description of them sounded interesting. Plus, she said she'd buy me lunch, so I was in.

After seeing the SMART Board, I was hooked. I decided it was just what my math class needed. What my students needed. What my shirt sleeves needed. What the school psychologist needed.

I thought that the use of the technology would make my lessons instantly more engaging. Plus, preparing lessons on my computer rather than on transparency sheets would be much more efficient and organized—and cleaner. I scheduled a meeting with my principal to request she purchase a Board for my classroom.

On the day of the meeting, I walked to her office with my notes about what I would say. I had a few pages full of case studies and statistics about SMART Boards, technology, and improving math scores. Fortunately, I did not pass the school psychologist on the way to the meeting. I doubt I would have made it there if I had walked past her.

Anyhow, after greeting the principal and sitting down, I said, "I attended a workshop about SMART Boards this summer."

Her response? "Oh! I love them! I've been wanting someone to pilot them for our school! Would you be interested?"

Could it really be that easy? "Yes! Of course I will!" I responded. I continued, "I actually prepared some notes complete with case studies and statistics to convince you that it would be a good purchase. Would you like to hear it?"

"No, please don't show them to me," she said with a laugh.

A few weeks later, I had a SMART Board in my room.

It turned out, I was mostly right. The SMART Board did make me more efficient. It did make it easier for me to prepare quality lessons for my class. My shirt sleeves were cleaner. The kids were more engaged because they enjoyed seeing me use the SMART Board. The school psychologist was even impressed with my new tech tool (and my lack of mysterious shirt sleeve stains).

But I was also a little wrong. My instruction improved, but this improvement wasn't *directly* caused by the addition of the SMART Board. I didn't realize it at first, but the Board had *indirectly* improved my instruction and student learning. Adding a SMART Board to bad teaching is not a certain ingredient for improvement. Adding a SMART Board to good teaching? That's got potential.

My instruction and my students' engagement and learning improved because using the SMART Board allowed me to be a more effective and efficient planner, and, therefore, teach better. Again, not because of the SMART Board, but because of what the SMART Board allowed me to do.

It's not about the technology that we teach with; it's about how we teach with the technology.

> It's not about the technology that we teach with; it's about how we teach with the technology.

My first observation of the school year was scheduled for a few weeks later. At the time, I thought, *This is going to be a sure thing. With the SMART Board, the principal is guaranteed to like my lesson.*

The next day, at our post-conference, she shared some of her feedback from the lesson. She praised me for a variety of teaching practices I had exhibited. To my surprise, though, she didn't mention the SMART Board once. After that meeting, I realized, you don't need an observer to be wowed by the technology you are using; you need the observer to be wowed by how you are using the technology.

You are being observed, not the technology.

> **You don't need an observer to be wowed by the technology you are using; you need the observer to be wowed by how you are using the technology.**

If someone observed me fixing the bounce house on that morning a few years back, they wouldn't be impressed by the duct tape, but they might be impressed by how I thought on my feet and saved the day for my kiddos.

People aren't impressed with my use of Camtasia; they're impressed with my ability to teach them a new skill in a forty-second GIF. Camtasia is just the tool that lets me do that.

The same was true with the SMART Board. It was an impressive tool, but what truly impressed my principal was how I used it to improve my craft as an educator.

Oh, I guess I left a bit of a cliffhanger in there. I know what you're wondering . . . *Did he ever remember to talk to the principal about that student issue?*

Yes, don't worry, as soon as I got back to my room, I remembered and returned to talk to the principal.

What's that? You feel like there was another cliffhanger? The school psychologist!? You'll have to tune in to Chapter 6 to find out how that story ends.

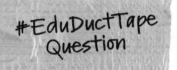
#EduDuctTape Question

How can my students blog about their learning and growth?

Online Resource Hub—EduDuctTape.com/hub/chapter05

BLOGGING TOOLS FOR REFLECTION

There's no doubt in my mind that reflecting on my experiences has helped me grow as an educator. Writing stories like the ones I've shared in this book helps me find the links and lessons. That's true for all of us. Reflection helps us make connections, recognize successes, and learn from failure. It's a powerful practice for educators, and it can be a powerful lever in our students' learning.

Philosopher, psychologist, and educational reformer John Dewey is often credited as saying, "We do not learn from experience. We learn from reflecting on experience." The experience itself is nothing without the reflection, and anything that we can do to enhance our students' reflection is sure to be beneficial. According to John Hattie, *evaluation and reflection* have an effect size of 0.75, placing the practices within the highest tier and indicating that they have the "potential to considerably accelerate student achievement."

For this question, which I could rewrite as "How can my students *reflect on* their learning and growth," we will focus on blogging. Blogs, originally known as *weblogs*, are online public (or semi-public) writing environments where the author's writing is typically displayed in reverse chronological order (most recent first). Most blogs allow readers to post comments to which authors can leave a reply. In some school settings, however, it may be necessary to limit or eliminate comments on the posts.

Blogs are a great example of focusing on what's *effective* rather than on what's *impressive*. Although most people associate blogs with the early 2000s and therefore would not be super impressed by one, a plethora of evidence indicates just how effective the practice can be.

For our students' development as writers, the positive impacts of blogging seem undeniable. In Hattie's work, *technology in writing* has an effect size of 0.42, placing it in the second highest tier. That term (technology in writing) is very vague and quite general, but blogging certainly fits it. In a *Journal of Adolescent & Adult Literacy* article in the early days of blogging—2002—Jo Ann Oravec, Professor of Information Technology at the University of Wisconsin at Whitewater, argued that developing weblogs can help students develop their own unique writing voice and "become more analytical and critical."

How can a student get better at writing? By writing! Blogs offer an opportunity for our students to write and add a touch of authenticity and novelty to the process. National Council of Teachers of English (NCTE) author Lisa Fink shared a quote from Traci Gardner, an instructor in the Department of English at Virginia Tech, stating, "When students write entries and comment on the entries of their peers, blogs become an integral part of a lively literacy community." A *lively literacy community*! What a great goal to have, and blogging may be the perfect vehicle to get us there.

Blogging in the classroom can also support students' development of important digital literacy and digital citizenship skills. Being part of one of these *lively literacy communities* teaches students so much. As a blog post on the PBLWorks site says, "If we are to empower students to take charge of their own learning and perform at high levels, having them publish professionally in the digital environment seems essential."

One of my favorite aspects of blogging in the classroom is that it provides what I call a *digital citizenship scaffold*. In other words, blogging within the safe confines of the classroom can give students experience in the digital world before they are expected to thrive in the "real world." Allowing students to develop their digital identities and experience the digital permanence of blogging within a walled garden or, if completely public, at least with the supervision of an educator, is akin to the driver's education courses and experiences that we recall from our teenage years. On more than one occasion during my early days behind the wheel, I was fortunate that my driving instructor had access to a passenger-side brake. Students would certainly also benefit from a *digital* passenger-side brake.

Writing and digital literacy are not the only educational reasons for blogging. Other benefits include providing the potential to increase our students' intrinsic motivation, giving them ownership over their learning, amplifying their voices, and connecting them with learners from around the world. Blogging about content and learning could also leverage the benefits of retrieval practice, which cognitive scientist Dr. Pooja Agarwal defines as a "strategy in which bringing information to mind enhances and boosts learning." In other words, we often have an easier time remembering things if we write about them.

Let's investigate a few tools that are appropriate for blogging in the learning environment.

Decide: Is this #EduDuctTape question (How can my students blog about their learning and growth?) one I need the answer to?

☐ **YES!** Continue below.   ☐ **NO!** Skim, if you'd like, then move on to the next chapter.

▶ **Think:** What would a blogging tool that's perfect **for me, my classroom, my students,** and **my content** look like? What does it need to do?

_____

_____

_____

_____

_____

Blogger

Blogger is a free tool that lives under the Google umbrella, though it's not part of the core of Google Workspace for Education. Many educators like Blogger because it may fit within the terms of service and privacy policies to which your school has already agreed. Blog-using educators like Blogger for its features. If your students use Blogger, they can do all of this:

- ✓ Select their own blog title and address (*youraddress*.blogspot.com).
- ✓ Select a theme.
- ✓ Set their blog as public, only seen by blog authors, or only seen by specified users, though those users must have Blogger accounts. (Public blogs can be hidden from search engine results.)
- ✓ Turn commenting on or off.
- ✓ Moderate comments before they are public.
- ✓ Use text, videos, images, and links in posts.
- ✓ Use embed code in posts to embed other digital content:
  - ▶ Google Slides
  - ▶ Audio files from Soundtrap or other sites
  - ▶ And more!

One downside of using a tool like Blogger is that it doesn't give you, as the teacher, any convenient control over your students' blogs.

Edublogs

Blogger is a good blogging platform that *could be* used within education, and Edublogs is a good blogging platform *made for* use in education. WordPress, which just so happens to be the most widely used content management system, powers Edublogs. Used by 40 percent of all websites, WordPress beats out other well-known options such as Squarespace, Wix, and Blogger, which each are used by fewer than 2 percent of all websites. Google Sites, by comparison, is used by less than 0.1 percent of all sites. What does that mean for you and your students? Well, it means with Edublogs you have a more capable platform than Blogger. But it's also a little more challenging to learn. More importantly, it means that by using Edublogs your students are learning a very marketable skill—using WordPress.

With Blogger, the feature list was a "The student can" list, but Edublogs gives *you* a robust set of student management tools:

- ✓ Moderate and approve content.
- ✓ Create student usernames and passwords so that blogs are not connected to your students' email addresses or names.
- ✓ Control privacy:
  - ▶ Viewable by anyone

- ▶ Viewable by Edublogs users
- ▶ Viewable by specific users
- ▶ Viewable by students from the same class
- ▶ Password-protected blogs (a great way to give families access!)

✓ Easily access all of your students' blogs.

✓ See all student activity in one location.

✓ Set it so that your students' new posts show up on a class blog as well as on their own.

What about from your *students'* perspective?

✓ They can use all of the essentials—text, videos, images, audio, and links—in their posts.

Ah, yes, of course you'd like to know about pricing. Most educators will be satisfied with the free version of Edublogs, but others may want to upgrade to a paid version to access its additional features:

★ More storage

★ Ability to embed HTML content (embed almost anything from the web!)

★ A variety of plugins, including some that can increase what can be shown on your site, such as Google Drive files

Write About

I need to warn you before I start this one. It's not a free tool and, aside from a trial version, there's no free option available. If you teach a writing or language arts class, you're going to want to know that up front, because I think that you're really going to like this tool. You're also going to want to keep reading to hear about why you should be interested in it even though it's not free.

First, let's look at Write About from your perspective. You can do several things with it:

✓ Assign students an *idea* (topics or story starters functioning like writing assignments).

✓ Suggest *idea* choices.

✓ Choose to let your students write freely.

✓ Select *ideas* from a curated collection.

✓ Include audio and images within the *idea* prompt.

✓ Include your own "mentor text" to model techniques and encourage new "writing moves."

✓ Send these *ideas* to specific groups, allowing for differentiation by ability, interest, or other needs that you've identified.

Before we look at the post-writing experience for you, let's look at Write About from your students' perspective. They can do all of this:

✓ Use the clear, easy-to-use interface.

✓ Take advantage of text-editing features.

✓ Add header images for each post as well as images within posts.

✓ Cite their sources for added images, as prompted by Write About.

✓ Add audio recordings to posts.

✓ Publish posts to you, a group, a class, their school, or to the public (if you have this enabled).

Finally, let's look at some of the after-writing features:

✓ You have three different ways to provide feedback on your students' writing:

    1. audio feedback

    2. text feedback

    3. in-text comments

✓ Your students see the feedback within Write About and can check them off after reading them.

✓ You see what comments have been "checked off" by the student.

✓ Your students can edit and repost their entry.

✓ You can approve the entry to be seen by other students in the class or in the school, or to be available to the public.

✓ Your students can add comments on each other's posts, unless you disable this.

✓ You can moderate comments before other students see them.

✓ You and your students can see some valuable data and graphs showing the student's number of posts, words written, and comments.

See, it's a good thing I told you it wasn't free up front. The cost, however, may just be worth it.

Fanschool

When I started writing this book, this section was about Kidblog. But not long before publication, I discovered (*Thanks for the heads up, Tony Vincent!*) that Kidblog had acquired two other edtech companies—Fanschool and InsertLearning—and would be known as just Fanschool. At the time of publication, it's not entirely clear how much Kidblog will change, but it appears that the existing features will likely remain.

Assuming that is the case, let's look at the features of Kidblog, which is a premium-only (read: *not free*) option that is comparable to Write About. First, let's look at what the teacher features allow you to do:

- ✓ Control your students' blog settings.
- ✓ Moderate who can view your students' posts as well as which posts are visible.
- ✓ Control who can comment and which comments are visible.
- ✓ Make private comments on blogs, which is a nice option for feedback.

The post creation settings for your students are also quite good and allow students to do the following:

- ✓ Include images, audio, video, uploaded files, and embedded objects from Google Drive (including Docs, Slides, and Drawings).
- ✓ Select to make posts viewable by you, their classmates, their *connections*, or anyone (you can customize the available options).
- ✓ Add comments that have all of the formatting features that a regular post has, including attaching images and Drive files.

The *connections* option is a nice way to start connecting your students with learners outside of their own classroom. This option lets teachers connect multiple classrooms so that the learners can share their work and writing with a wider audience.

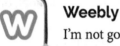

Weebly

I'm not going to lie: I chuckled a little when I saw someone suggest Weebly for student blogs. My thought was "What is it, 2007!?" And I was half right. Many aspects of Weebly have not kept up with the rest of the internet. But I was also half wrong. Weebly offers a pretty good option for classroom blogging.

The free Weebly for Education plans allow you to do the following:

- ✓ Create your own site.
- ✓ Create sites for up to forty students.

Their free sites have a number of features:

- ✓ Sites can have up to five pages.
- ✓ Accounts don't require any personally identifiable information.
- ✓ You can administer your students' accounts and even disable their editing or delete their sites if needed.

✓ Students can drag and drop different elements into pages.

✓ Elements can contain text, images, YouTube videos, file attachments, and HTML embed code, along with a few other options.

✓ Student Weebly sites can be set as public or private with a password so that designated viewers (parents, teachers, classmates) can access the site.

✓ Each individual blog post can have comments turned on, off, or on with approvals required.

Weebly Education Pro accounts adds in the following capabilities:

★ You can make more student accounts.

★ Your students can make more sites and more pages per site.

★ Your students can upload larger files.

★ Your students can embed videos and audio.

★ Your students can password-protect pages.

Gimkit Ink

It should come as no surprise that the same team that flipped the script on formative assessment review games with Gimkit is also taking a fresh approach to student publishing. If the previously mentioned options don't work for you, this might be what you need.

Ink typically starts with you creating a project. You can:

✓ Assign projects that are prompts, topics, questions, a certain day or week, or whatever you choose!

✓ Include videos, graphs, images, and more in the details.

✓ Choose who can respond: anyone with the link or students in certain classes.

✓ Choose who can view completed posts: anyone with the link or just classmates.

When your students respond to the project, they can choose to respond in an *article* format or in a slideshow-like *stories* format. For the most part, what they can do within their post is the same with each option:

✓ Your students can include just about anything off the web within their *article* or *story*: including Desmos Graphs, YouTube Videos, Scratch Projects, and Google Docs, Sheets, and Slides.

✓ Your students can also post *solos*: stories or articles that are not a part of a specific project.

Now, the important part comes when your students press that *publish* button:

✓ You can see all completed student posts, and your students can choose whether to make the posts visible to their classmates as well as whether their name is included.

✓ Your students can make their posts more private than you selected, but they cannot make it less private. In other words, if you set a project as public, your students can still opt for their own response to be private.

✓ Once posted, your students' posts show up alongside other student posts within the same project.

✓ In terms of feedback, you and your students can comment on their posts, but their classmates cannot.

Finally, because Gimkit has to pay the bills somehow, there is one reason that you might want to consider the pro version of Gimkit Ink. Although the basic version has all of the functionality, it limits you to ten projects. You'll need to upload to the pro version to use an unlimited number of projects.

There are more!?

That's right; there are lots of options here. Some of the simpler options include Docs/Word, Slides/PowerPoint, and Google Classroom/Microsoft Teams. Many educators swear by these options because of the familiarity and safety they offer. Other learning management systems, such as Schoology, also offer a built-in blogging option. Seesaw gives your students the ability to post to a class-shared blog to which all of the students in the class contribute. Wix, the fifth most common application for website creation, is also in the process of rolling out an education version that offers teacher moderation, feedback, and other features. A variety of other worthy options, such as Wakelet, Adobe Spark Pages, Padlet, and Bulb, also are available.

DECISION TIME!

Are you going to try out one of these tools?   ☐ Yes   ☐ No

Which one(s)?

☐ Blogger
☐ Edublogs
☐ Write About
☐ Fanschool (Kidblog)

☐ Weebly
☐ Gimkit Ink
☐ Something else: _____

When are you going to try it out?

☐ Do Now   ☐ Do Soon   ☐ Do Later

Is there a certain lesson, activity, topic, or unit you'll use it for?

_____

_____

If it might solve a problem or meet one of your goals, it's worth committing to trying it out!

Don't forget to check out the resources and tutorials at the Online Resource Hub! There's probably a video about using the tool that you've selected!

(EduDuctTape.com/hub/chapter05)

RAMEN NOODLES, LONELY NIGHTS, AND LOUD KIDS

I had tried the chicken-flavored Maruchan-brand ramen noodle. I had tried the beef-flavored Maruchan-brand ramen noodle. I had tried mixing them together. I had even tried some of the less-common flavors. I was running out of options. But I didn't have money for much else.

During my last semester of college, I had to quit my part-time job to focus on my student teaching, applications for teaching positions, and my coursework. So, I was running short on money. And so, I ate lots of the fifteen-cent packs of ramen noodles. This experience motivated me to get a job with a school as quickly as possible. No year of substitute teaching for me. I needed to get into the classroom.

And so, by the time August rolled around, I was starting a job as a math teacher. It was the perfect solution to my ramen noodle problem: I needed to earn money, so I found a solution (a full-time job teaching at a local public school).

A few years before that, I had a different problem. I was attending undergraduate mechanical engineering classes at the University of Akron and I was just "not feeling it." I was bored, uninspired, and unengaged. I could not imagine myself working in that field for years. I also had an itch to do something different. That itch started years earlier, when my high school math teacher gave me the opportunity to tutor elementary students who were struggling with math: I wanted to work with kids.

Consequently, by the time the next semester started, I had switched majors from mechanical engineering to education. I had a problem: I wanted to change my career path to one working with kids, so I found a solution (changing my major to education).

While I was working as a math teacher, I had a new problem. We've already discussed this problem: too much content, too many transparency markers, and too much Vis-a-Vis marker ink on my shirt sleeves. We've also already discussed the solution: a SMART Board.

This SMART Board problem ran concurrent to another problem: I was getting lonely. I needed a companion. So, I found a solution: I asked the aforementioned school psychologist out on a date. April—the school psychologist—and I have been married for more than fourteen years. Problem. Solution.

April and I really enjoyed the newlywed life at first. Dinners with friends, afternoon movies, meals in front of the TV, sleeping in, happy hours after work, long hikes, and more. But we had a set of problems. We had too much flexibility. We had too much free time. Our house was too quiet. We were tired of being able to do whatever we wanted, whenever we wanted (*Could I be more sarcastic?*). So we implemented a series of solutions. A Boston Terrier named Kermit the Dog came first. Later, our son Cohen, followed by our daughter Parker. And then, just for good measure, our youngest son, Beckett. Problems: solved.

THE PROBLEM–SOLUTION PATTERN

If you look at all of these anecdotes, except for the last one, which was a little silly and "tongue-in-cheek," they all follow a *problem–solution* pattern. This all runs parallel to the Educational Duct Tape idea. Focus on problems, goals, or needs, and identify things you can do to solve them.

I'm not trying to impress you with my skills as a problem-solver (*Look at me! When I was a broke college kid, I ate lots of ramen noodle!*), I'm trying to sell you on a technology integration mindset. I'm trying to do that because I know how overwhelming the plethora of educational technology options can be. I've sat in plenty of faculty meetings, mandatory professional developments, and conferences. I know how you feel. And I know the solution: identify your problems, goals, or needs and then figure out how educational technology can help.

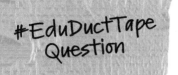
#EduDuctTape Question

How can my students self-assess their learning?

Online Resource Hub—EduDuctTape.com/hub/chapter06

If we're going to apply a *problem–solution* strategy to our practice as educators, we must reflect on our practice as educators and self-assess our areas of success and growth.

It is also beneficial for our *students* to reflect and self-assess throughout the learning experience. Paul Black and Dylan William state that self-assessment is "a *sine qua non* for effective learning." This translates literally as "Without which, not," which is to say, "Without this, the other thing won't be possible." In other words, without self-assessment, effective learning would not be possible.

Student self-assessment takes the students from assessment **of** learning (summative assessments) beyond assessment **for** learning (formative assessments) to assessment **as** learning. In other words, the students learn about their own knowledge, skills, performance, and abilities from this process.

In their article, "Student Self-Assessment: The Key to Stronger Student Motivation and Higher Achievement," James McMillan and Jessica Hearn explain that "self-assessment occurs when students judge their own work to improve performance as they identify discrepancies between current and desired performance."

If we relate the elements outlined in that quote back to John Hattie's research from *Visible Learning*, we can see connections to highly beneficial classroom practices.

Quality self-assessment should connect to students' *self-efficacy*, which Hattie found to have 0.92 effect size—the eleventh highest of the 256 factors covered in his 2018 update to his data. This means self-efficacy—a person's belief in their own abilities—has the "potential to considerably accelerate student achievement," placing it within Hattie's highest level of influences on student achievement.

Even more promising, if we have our students predict their own performance and establish their own learning goals, we are leveraging an even more powerful influence on student achievement: *self-reported grades*, which Hattie has measured to have a 1.33 effect size. This is the second highest in his 2018 data.

Finally, Hattie's work also consistently shows motivation falling above the 0.4 effect size hinge point. And if self-assessment increases motivation, which I believe it does, this is further evidence in self-assessment's favor.

McMillan and Hearn identified three stages to the self-assessment cycle: self-monitoring, self-evaluation, and identifying learning targets and instructional correctives. Let's look at some educational technology tools that can play a role in the self-evaluation stage. Many are often thought of as formative assessment tools, but they also can be beneficial pieces of the self-assessment process.

TOOLS FOR SELF-ASSESSMENT

Note that just using one of these tools does not mean you are guaranteed to tap into those effect sizes Hattie reported or that *sine qua non* Black and William mentioned. However, these tools can do one important part: telling your students when and what they are and are not comprehending.

> **Decide:** Is this #EduDuctTape question (How can my students self-assess their learning?) one I need the answer to?
>
> ☐ **YES!** Continue below.   ☐ **NO!** Skim, if you'd like, then move on to the next chapter.

▶ **Think:** What would a self-assessment tool that's perfect **for me, my classroom, my students,** and **my content** look like? What does it need to do?

_____

_____

_____

_____

_____

You're right! You're wrong!

Let's start off with tools that enable the most basic element of self-assessment: your students knowing whether they're right or wrong. Most, but not all, of the formative assessment tools we discussed in earlier chapters fall into this category of self-assessment.

Fitting into this category are Quizizz, Quizlet, Blooket, Kahoot, Quizalize, Formative, Socrative, Poll Everywhere, and Plickers, among others. In each of these platforms, your students either will see whether they were correct *on their own screen* or will see the correct answer—enabling self-checking—*on your screen*. Note that some of these platforms have question types that don't autograde and, therefore, don't automatically give your students the information necessary for self-assessing.

 Quizizz adds in a few bonuses in terms of self-assessment.

✓ Your students will be prompted to slow down if they are quickly answering questions incorrectly.

✓ At the end of the game, your students will have the opportunity to reattempt one missed question—a *redemption question*—which gives them the opportunity to see growth.

✓ Your students can play games more than once.

✓ Your students can practice with *flashcards* mode.

Quizlet has multiple features that support self-assessment:

- ✓ Their most basic feature—*flashcards*—is all self-assessment.
- ✓ *Learn* mode directs your students to repeat each question until they answer it correctly two times, causing them to pay closer attention to their performance on certain questions.

✓ The three other *study* modes (*write, spell,* and *test*) ask your students to answer a question and then confirm whether they were correct.

✓ The two *play* modes (*match* and *gravity*) will let your students know whether they're correct.

Kahoot offers a set of *study* modes that your students can leverage for self-assessment.

- ✓ *Flashcards* mode turns your Kahoot into the original self-assessment tool.
- ✓ *Practice* mode puts your student in a single-person version of a regular Kahoot game.

✓ *Test yourself* mode shows your students their scores, potentially motivating them to play the games repeatedly to achieve their ideal scores. Any time students are trying to get better at something, they are tapping into self-assessment.

✓ *Personalized learning* mode, a premium feature, prompts your students to review questions they missed after the game is over. Although we certainly hope to empower students to drive their own path with self-assessment, this prompt could provide a helpful nudge.

2 Fast, 2 Furious?

You may notice I left Gimkit and Blooket out of the list above. While students' excitement about the gameplay made them edtech darlings (my favorite proof is a tweet from @MrCarlsonsClass that said, "*Umm* so my students just asked for vocabulary review with @gimkit during recess. Please advise."), one thing Gimkit and Blooket could have more of is self-assessment.

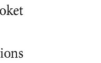

As with the tools listed above, your students *can* see whether they got questions right or wrong (assuming you haven't disabled that feature in Gimkit), but Gimkit and Blooket games move so fast, they may not fully process that feedback. At the end of the game, your students see what their final score or dollar amount was, but there's no information about their actual academic performance.

So, what do we do? Students love playing Gimkit and Blooket, you get some formative assessment data, and almost everyone ends the game with a smile on their face . . . but we wish they had better self-assessment features. It all comes down to what your goals are. If fun formative assessment and review are major aspects of those goals, then you might be willing to accept this decreased amount of self-assessment.

Good Ol' Flashcards

Back in my day, we walked two miles, in the snow, uphill both ways, to buy index cards so we could self-assess our learning. Flashcards are still worth leveraging in certain situations and, therefore, some tech tools leverage it. (By the way, according to Dr. Jared Cooney Horvath, brain science has shown it's best to review the whole deck again, rather than moving correct ones to a "done" pile.)

The O.G. (*Original Gangsta!*) of technological flashcards is Quizlet. In Quizlet's regular flashcard mode, the site does not check whether your students are right or wrong or ask them to confirm whether they were, but the student has the chance to determine this on their own. This may actually be a more powerful self-assessment factor.

Some of the other tools also have a flashcards option. Both Quizizz and Kahoot offer flashcards options that prompt students to self-assess and review cards they struggled with.

Flippity.net

One of my favorite tools for digital flashcards is Flippity.net. This tool creates a variety of interactive tools from Google Sheets. If that sounds intimidating, don't worry. Simply make a copy of an available template on their site, add your content, and click a link. Easy-peasy! Flippity Flashcards offers a variety of beneficial features:

- ✓ Your students can click a button to have both sides of the card read aloud to them.
- ✓ Your students can remove cards after mastering them. Again, best practice is to repeat those cards too, but sometimes it can be helpful to remove them.
- ✓ Your students can shuffle the stack.
- ✓ Your students can flip the stack so that the front and back of the card switch places.
- ✓ You can add pictures and videos to your flashcards!

Another benefit of using Flippity.net is that you can turn those same spreadsheets into a variety of other self-assessment and formative assessment tools, including these:

- ✓ Scavenger hunt
- ✓ Board game
- ✓ Matching game
- ✓ Click-and-drag manipulatives
- ✓ Bingo
- ✓ Word search
- ✓ Word scramble (also known as a word jumble)
- ✓ Crossword puzzle
- ✓ Snowman (like Hangman)
- ✓ Quiz show (like Jeopardy)
- ✓ Word cloud

Spreadsheet Conditional Formatting

If you knew me before picking up this book, you probably knew I love spreadsheets almost as much as I love my wife, kids, family, coffee, and beer. My spreadsheet tool of choice is Google Sheets, but for this use, it probably doesn't matter which you use. In terms of self-assessment, I think spreadsheets' conditional formatting feature can be really useful.

In Google Sheets, for example, you could add a question in one cell (*let's go with, "How do you pronounce GIF?"*) and then leave a cell for your students to type in their answer (*let's hope they write "With a Hard G."*). Then, you can navigate to *Format > Conditional Formatting* and set the cell to turn green if the correct answer (*"With a Hard G."*) is typed into the cell. You could even set it to turn red if anything *other than* the correct answer is typed in (*"With a Soft G."*).

Conditional formatting might scare off some educators because they're not comfortable with spreadsheets. However, imagine the power of sending out a spreadsheet like this through Google Classroom, or your learning management system of choice, so your students can check their own answers to important questions! There's a lot of potential there.

I should note, by the way, that although my example is funny (to me, at least), it's not an ideal one. The cell will only turn green for the phrase "With a Hard G," so if my student gives a different correct answer (*"Hard G,"* or *"Like gift."*), it won't turn green. Therefore, this is only good for questions with one clear, correct answer or if you use data validation to create a multiple-choice dropdown.

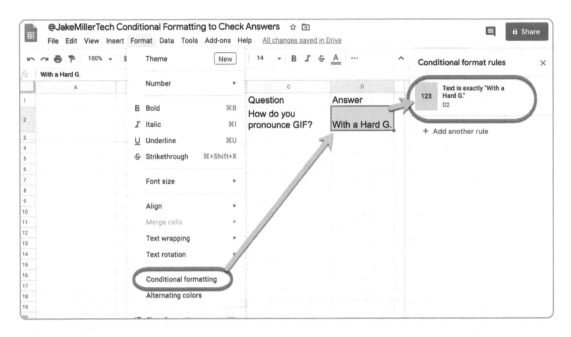

Another possible issue with this suggestion is, if your students know how to, they can actually go into the conditional formatting settings and find the correct answer. So, it's important you only use this for self-assessment, not for an important formative or summative assessment.

Spreadsheet Checklists

While we're on the topic of spreadsheets, another option is to create—or have your students create—a skills checklist in a spreadsheet. The tools above support the self-evaluation state of McMillan and Hearn's self-assessment cycle, but this could support another stage: self-monitoring. Because our earlier quote tells us, "Self-assessment occurs when students judge their own work," a system that helps them organize those judgments and prioritize next steps could be beneficial.

Imagine writing, "Put fractions in order on a number line" in one cell and then, in the neighboring cell, a checkbox for the student to check off when they have mastered the skill. In Google Sheets, click *Insert > Checkbox* to add that box. In Microsoft Excel, this feature is not as conveniently accessed, but you could use something else—like an *x* or checkmark symbol—to mimic a checkbox.

Then, if you provide your students with a copy of that spreadsheet, they can check things off as they master them. If you want to get really fancy, you can even use conditional formatting (see the previous topic) to color code those cells when they are mastered!

If you're intimidated by the spreadsheets idea, you can now build functional checklists in Google Docs as well.

Note: You could also use a similar system as the teacher as a formative assessment piece. That spreadsheet will help you know which students have (or have not) mastered certain skills, thus helping you plan next steps.

Wait, that's not all of them!?

Most of the tools covered in this section help students self-assess by autograding them. This is a helpful feature, but a more beneficial one would be to have your students actually *assess* their comprehension and skill. For that reason, just as any tool can be a formative assessment tool, any tool can also be a self-assessment tool, *if* the students reflect on their product or answer and assess their performance.

Keep in mind that some of these tools focus on performance goals—getting all of the answers right—rather than on mastery goals—improving knowledge. You may therefore choose to supplement these tools with features that promote a mastery orientation through metacognitive activities such as reflecting on their growth. This is one practice that, if done right, could promote a mastery orientation is the use of rubrics, but that's a different #EduDuctTape question!

DECISION TIME!

Are you going to try out one of these tools? ☐ Yes ☐ No

Which one(s)?

☐ Quizizz
☐ Quizlet
☐ Kahoot
☐ Quizalize
☐ Formative
☐ Socrative
☐ Poll Everywhere
☐ Plickers

☐ Gimkit
☐ Quizlet flashcards
☐ Quizizz flashcards
☐ Kahoot flashcards
☐ Flippity.net
☐ Spreadsheet conditional formatting
☐ Checklists
☐ Something else: _____

When are you going to try it out?

☐ Do Now   ☐ Do Soon   ☐ Do Later

Is there a certain lesson, activity, topic, or unit you'll use it for?

_____

_____

If it might solve a problem or meet one of your goals, it's worth committing to trying it out!

Don't forget to check out the resources and tutorials at the Online Resource Hub! There's probably a video about using the tool that you've selected!

(EduDuctTape.com/hub/chapter06)

SEVEN

EIGHT MINUTES, CRAZY SOLUTIONS, AND TALKING TO MYSELF

I was having a full-on teacher nervous breakdown. This was a big problem. While sitting at a bar one night, I told my college friends about it. Most of them were mechanical engineers. They didn't get it. It didn't seem like a problem to them. Actually, it kind of seemed like a bonus in their eyes. But when I told my teacher friends? They got it. When I talk about this during workshops or presentations, the educators in attendance are on the edge of their seats.

What was the problem? Eight minutes. Our school schedule was changing, and each of our class periods would be eight minutes shorter than they were the previous year.

It was my third year in that role. Remember, the first year was my transparency markers and overhead projector year. The second year was my SMART Board year. The third year was supposed to be the year all of that paid off. The year I opened those SMART Notebook files from the previous year, tweaked them as needed, and benefited from the time spent on those lessons in the previous year.

But if the class periods were all eight minutes shorter, those lessons would never work. Each lesson would need to be modified to fit into eight fewer minutes. It's not like I could just push content back because I'd run out of time at the end of the year. I needed a solution.

I thought about lots of solutions.

- Stop learning the kids' names. I spend so much time learning them and saying them!
- Stop greeting the kids as they enter the room. This takes a few minutes each day!
- Stop talking to the class before starting the lesson. Who needs rapport and relationships? Just launch right into it!
- Start teaching while kids walk in. No time to sit down; you'd better start listening on your way in!

- Stop going over the homework. Hopefully, they understood it all. And if not? It's their problem! I don't have time to go over it!
- No more assessments. I don't have time to reteach, so why even assess!?

As you can tell, none of these solutions was a good fit. But then, I started to think about the technologies I had available to me. I had a laptop, I had a SMART Board, and I had recently learned about screencasting. I had never tried screencasting because I hadn't identified a need for it, but I knew it was possible.

Instead of starting class by taking attendance, then talking to kids who had been absent, and then going over the homework, what if I could do them all at the same time? I realized if I put these three things together—the laptop, SMART Board, and screencasting—I could.

Each day, during my planning period, I would turn on my projector, open up an image of the day's homework, start my screen recording software, and do the homework. I would record a five- to eight-minute-long video of myself doing the homework.

My colleagues probably thought I was crazy! I assume they walked by my room and saw me at my SMART Board, talking in my teacher voice and solving math problems . . . to an empty classroom.

Teacher 1: "Man, Miller really loves teaching math. He even does it when he doesn't have students!"

Teacher 2: "Is he pretend-teaching about solving equations again today!?"

Teacher 1: "Yup, it seems like he's really into them."

The next day, once my students were in their seats, I would play that video. You can go to this link (eduducttape.com/MathHWVideo) to see an example, but you can probably imagine what they were watching. The video showed what was on the SMART Board at the time of the recording, along with any drawing or writing I did, and the video included my voice. It was like I was at the board going over the homework . . . except, I wasn't. I was circulating around the classroom, taking attendance, giving students grades based on whether they had completed their assignment and showed their work (*I am embarrassed to admit this*), checking in with students who were absent the previous day, and preparing information for students who were absent on that day.

But that wasn't all I was doing. Those were the things I thought I would accomplish during that time, but I actually accomplished much more: I was seeing which students were marking lots of things incorrect and might need some peer-tutoring later.

I was seeing which students were feeling confident, were comprehending the skills, and would make good peer tutors later in class.

I was seeing which students seemed frustrated and would need support later.

I was seeing which students had different strategies I could spotlight later.

I was seeing what common mistakes I needed to go over.

I had designed my little hack to make up for an eight-minute time difference, but it also enabled me to do multiple types of formative assessments.

And it was all thanks to the technology. *Wait, that's not right.* It was all thanks to *how I used* the technology.

SMART Boards, screencasts, and video added to **bad** teaching is, essentially, putting lipstick on a pig. (*My apologies if you think pigs are adorable.*)

SMART Boards, screencasts, and video added to **good** teaching practices, observations of what students need, and reflection on how practices are impacting students? That's like putting lipstick on . . . *um*, the school psychologist.

By viewing the technologies—a laptop, a SMART Board, and screencasting software—as tools, I was able to use them to solve a problem I had in my classroom. As often happens, I found that using technology this way also solved problems and met goals I didn't even know I had. I hadn't realized that going over the homework at the front of the room was keeping me from knowing how my students were performing. I hadn't realized I was missing out on some key formative assessment opportunities.

Educational technology is at its most useful when it is not the goal of the lesson but a tool used to solve a problem, meet a goal, or address a learning standard!

How can my students and I record screencasts for flipped lessons or blended learning?

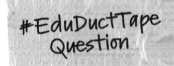
#EduDuctTape
Question

Online Resource Hub—EduDuctTape.com/hub/chapter07

Decide: Is this #EduDuctTape question (above) one I need the answer to?

☐ **YES!** Continue below.　　☐ **NO!** Skim, if you'd like, then
　　　　　　　　　　　　　　　　　move on to the next chapter.

> ► **Think:** What would a screencasting tool that's perfect **for me, my classroom, my students,** and **my content** look like? What does it need to do?

_____

_____

_____

_____

▨ TOOLS FOR SCREENCASTING

The duct tape I used when I needed to make up for that loss of eight minutes was a screencasting program called Jing. Jing is still technically available, but it's no longer a commonly used screencasting program. Let's look at a few of the contemporary options and then, more importantly, think about them from an educational duct tape perspective.

One major difference between the tools we'll discuss is the length of the videos you can create. It's important to keep in mind that studies have shown engagement in instructional videos drops slightly at six to nine minutes and drastically in videos longer than nine minutes. So, even though we'd love to record an entire lesson, there is clear evidence doing so is not best pedagogical practice.

Screencastify

According to their website, Screencastify is the "No. 1 Screen Recorder for Chrome." And there's a handful of good reasons for that:

✓ It's easy to use.

✓ The free version is sufficient.

✓ It syncs to Google Drive.

✓ Videos are not stored on Screencastify's servers.

And that's not all! In the free version you can:

✓ Record your screen, webcam, or both.

✓ Export videos that are up to five minutes long.

✓ Record an unlimited number of videos.

✓ Record while offline.

✓ Add cursor effects, including a spotlight, a click circle, or even fireworks when you click.

- ✓ Use pen, eraser, and rectangle tools to annotate on your screen.
- ✓ Add emojis to your recordings.
- ✓ Easily upload to YouTube, EdPuzzle, Google Classroom, and more.
- ✓ Export your recordings as videos, GIFs, or MP3s.
- ✓ Trim, cut, or split your videos.
- ✓ Add customizable text over your clips.
- ✓ Zoom in or crop out parts of your recordings.
- ✓ Merge videos together (up to five minutes total).
- ✓ Record tab audio as part of your videos.
- ✓ Edit the audio levels.
- ✓ Toggle between different cameras mid-recording.
- ✓ Add blurring over sensitive or distracting information in your recording.

The features listed above are all a part of the free version. There are "Unlimited" paid versions for each of element of their tools (*Record*, *Edit*, and *Submit*), which all add in one important additional feature:

★ Unlimited video lengths! ★

In 2020, Screencastify also added Screencastify Submit, which creates a convenient system for you to request and collect video submissions from your students. You send a link to your students, they record from any device, and the video auto-magically appears in your Google Drive! And, if you assign them through as Google Classroom assignments, you'll be able to leverage their feedback, grading, and organizational features! Screencastify Submit has minimal recording and editing features, but the streamlined process for video assignments is great! In the free version, you can have one active assignment at a time, but in the paid version you can have unlimited active assignments.

In 2021, Screencastify announced some pedagogical additions to the tool. These include the ability to ask auto-graded, multiple-choice questions and to see which students have watched your videos. More on this later!

Screencast-O-Matic

This tool has been trusted by Windows PC users for years but added in web-based recording a few years ago. That means it can now record on Chromebooks along with Macs and Windows PCs. Much like Screencastify, Screencast-O-Matic has an easy-to-use free version that's worth considering. With it you can do the following:

✓ Record screen, webcam, or both.

✓ Export videos that are up to fifteen minutes long (or unlimited lengths for mobile recordings).

✓ Record an unlimited number of videos.

✓ Add captions to your videos by uploading them.

✓ Select from a supply of stock music files to add to your videos.

Recently, Screencast-O-Matic added mobile and Chromebook versions that have extra free capabilities:

✓ Adding text, sticker, and image overlays

✓ Utilizing filters and effects

✓ Adjusting video speed

✓ Rotating and cropping video

✓ Trimming portions of video

✓ Adding narration

Their inexpensive "Deluxe" paid version adds some features to their desktop version:

★ Unlimited video lengths

★ Green screen filter

★ Automated speech-to-text captioning

★ Narration or music importing

★ An expanded collection of stock music files

★ Overlay insertion

★ Transitions insertion

★ Video speed modification (speed up or slow down)

★ Pen tool

★ System audio recording

★ Zooming in

Aside from the time limit and captioning, though, Screencastify's free version beats out Screencast-O-Matic's in almost every other column (especially the pen tool, Google Drive sync,

GIF export, and audio export). If you're willing to pay, though, Screencast-O-Matic's paid version adds in quite a few features that might make it the tool for you.

Loom

You know that feeling when someone tells you their favorite taco joint has better tacos than your favorite taco spot? And then it turns out they have a point? Is this an issue that only I deal with? Maybe. Maybe this is a loose metaphor, but I like tacos, okay!?

Well, this happened to me with screencasting programs. I had been recommending my favorite taco joint . . . *er* . . . screen recording program—Screencastify—to teachers who had used Google (*G Suite!? Google Apps for Education!? GAFE!? Google Workspace?*) for years. And when someone told me they preferred Loom, I was like, "*Girl, please.*" But then I researched it and found out they had a point. My favorite taco spot—Screencastify—is still great, but it turns out their favorite taco spot—Loom—makes a pretty darn good barbacoa taco . . . *er* . . . screen recording.

The free *Loom for Education* accounts contain most of Loom's Pro features. With those accounts, you can do the following:

- ✓ Record videos that are up to forty-five minutes long.
- ✓ Record your screen, webcam, or both.
- ✓ Record an unlimited number of videos.
- ✓ Trim or cut parts of your videos.
- ✓ Use the popular circular webcam window.
- ✓ Add a call-to-action button to insert a link.
- ✓ Record screen or camera videos from your iOS phone or device with the iOS app.
- ✓ Record screen or screen with camera videos from your Android phone with the Android app.
- ✓ See emoji reactions and time-stamped comments from your viewers.
- ✓ Password-protect your videos.
- ✓ See who viewed the video (if they have an account).
- ✓ Record tab audio (coming soon: system audio).
- ✓ Organize all your videos into folders.
- ✓ Toggle between cameras mid-recording.

A few features are only available in the desktop version (Mac or Windows):

✓ Click Highlighting

✓ Pen Tool

One of my favorite local taco spots only uses corn tortillas. My wife and I love them, but my oldest son does not. Screen recorders and other tech tools are similar. Certain cons to tools impact some users more than others. While we love Loom's free higher recording limit, it does have a few corn tortilla features. The first is that it's not easy to get your Loom videos into Google Drive or YouTube. It's possible, but you've got to download them from Loom and then upload them to the other service. It's also lacking two of Screencastify's big features: exporting as GIFs and as audio files. When compared with Screencast-O-Matic's free version, Loom is a pretty clear winner, aside from captioning (which Loom lists as a feature that is coming soon). Screencast-O-Matic's paid version, however, has more extensive editing options.

I'm going to go have some tacos. brb.

Flipgrid

Flipgrid again!? Yup! On April 1, 2020, Flipgrid announced the addition of screen recording to their platform. And it wasn't an April Fools' Day joke!

If you click the *options* button while recording a video in Flipgrid, you'll see some other options. One of those options is *Record Screen*. These videos can be part of a topic's prompt, part of a response, or even a standalone Flipgrid Short. They're easy to use, and numerous:

✓ Record videos that are up to ten minutes long.

✓ Trim or cut parts of your videos.

✓ Combine multiple clips.

✓ Rearrange clips.

✓ Take advantage of automatic captioning.

✓ Edit the auto-captions.

✓ Add music to your recordings (coming Fall 2021).

✓ Combine screen recordings with

▶ webcam-only recordings

▶ recordings that use Flipgrid's whiteboard or blackboard background

▶ videos saved to your computer

✓ Share or embed your recordings.

✓ Download your videos.

The flexibility screen recording offers combined with the convenience factor if you're already a Flipgrid user make this tool a great choice. The only major downsides for this tool are the ten-minute recording limit and the lack of during-recording annotation tools. But if those aren't super important to you, this is a great option!

> Now, I could easily stop this list right here and know I gave you exactly what you paid for *(assuming you didn't steal this book . . . you didn't, did you!?)*. Honestly, those four pretty effectively cover the main screencasting options in K–12 educational technology. But I've been an overachiever all of my life, so I'm going to share three more, just for good measure. Why am I separating these three from the rest of the pack? Well, they're bigger and more fully featured than the others . . . but that might be just what you need!

WeVideo

There are two parts to WeVideo. First up is their Quick Recorder extension for Chrome or Edge. This free tool only works on educator accounts and gives you plenty of functions:

- ✓ Record your screen, webcam, or both.
- ✓ Use the pen tool to annotate your recordings.
- ✓ Turn on cursor and click highlighting.
- ✓ Download your videos or upload them to Google Drive or OneDrive.
- ✓ Record an unlimited number of videos that are up to five minutes long.

The second part of WeVideo reminds me of our Vitamix. When I initially researched it, I discovered it was a great high-performance blender. In my research, I also discovered it could be used for making soups, ice creams, and more! Guess how many times we've used it for soup. If you guessed 0, you're right. Guess how many times we've used it for ice cream. Again, 0.

Anyhow, WeVideo is a bit like our Vitamix, except for the fact I think you'd use *all* of this online video editor's features, even the soup and ice cream options!

The catch here is that there are limitations if you use the screencasting option in a WeVideo free plan. You can:

- ✓ Record unlimited five-minute-long videos in the aforementioned extension or longer videos from within their editor.

✓ Record your screen *or* webcam, but not both at the same time in the editor. You can also do screen *and* webcam in the extension.

✓ Access and edit your videos from any device.

✓ Add royalty-free music to your recordings.

✓ Edit the videos that you record with the browser extension.

There are two limitations on the WeVideo free plan:

✓ Your videos made within the editor are watermarked. Videos recorded with the extension are not, unless you edit them in the editor.

✓ WeVideo limits you to 1 GB cloud storage space. You can download videos recorded with the extension or save them to Google Drive or OneDrive so that they don't count against this limit.

Wait, wait, wait, don't skip to the next section yet! While you might not want to pay for a screencasting tool, you might want to pay for a video editor for other projects or classes. And, if you're paying for WeVideo for those uses, then you might as well use it for screencasting, too! Here's what you get in the paid version:

★ A full-featured video editor

★ 50 GB of cloud storage

★ Standard HD video resolution

★ The ability to edit in these ways:

  ▶ Change the size of your recording.

  ▶ Crop the recording.

  ▶ Layer content.

  ▶ Change audio levels and add audio.

  ▶ Add transitions, animations, and annotations.

  ▶ Adjust the speed of the video.

Did you know that a Vitamix can also make dips, nut butters, and baby food? It's true. Did you know that WeVideo provides other stuff too? Also true! WeVideo provides these:

★ Hundreds of thousands of commercially licensed, royalty-free stock video, audio, and images

★ Green screen video creation

★ Collaboration between creators

★ Easy export to the most important platforms (YouTube, Google Drive, DropBox, Microsoft OneDrive, etc.)

I don't know about you, but I'd rather create a really rad screencast than a nut butter any day. From a screencasting perspective, these are my five favorite features in the WeVideo editor:

1. The screencast and webcam video are separate tracks, so you can make edits to each.
2. You can green screen yourself into the screencast instead of being trapped in that little rectangle or circle.
3. You can add tons of annotations.
4. You can speed up or slow down parts of the screencast.
5. You can easily add a voiceover to your screencast.

And, finally, in the WeVideo for Schools version, you can create video assignments for your students and see and manage their recordings.

I wonder if I could make a good taco with our Vitamix. . . .

RecordCast

Want some of those fancy Vitamix-level editing features in a free package? Check out RecordCast, a new tool that looks really promising, and more importantly, really free. In this easy-to-use free tool you can do several things:

✓ Record videos that are up to thirty minutes long.
✓ Record your screen, webcam, or both.
✓ Actively work on up to eight video projects.
✓ Once you export a video, you can remove it and free up a spot.
✓ Record system audio.
✓ Record without any installs or browser extensions.
✓ Download your videos as an MP4 *if* you use the editor.
✓ Add text overlays, titles, and transitions.
✓ Edit audio, webcam, and your screen recording separately with the multitrack editor.
✓ Import audio, images, and videos into your projects.
✓ Zoom in and crop your recordings.
✓ Split, trim, and cut from your recordings.

Camtasia

If WeVideo is the Vitamix of screen recorders, then Camtasia is the . . . um, I don't know. They'd be whatever machine some fancy smoothie and juice shop uses. As I mentioned back in Chapter 2, Camtasia is the screencasting tool I use. It has every feature you need in a screen recorder except for two. First, it's not web-based, and therefore it doesn't work on Chromebooks, mobile devices, or tablets.

The other issue with Camtasia is its price tag. It's going to cost more than the aforementioned tools combined. If you're hoping to become the next creator of YouTube tutorials or online video courses, Camtasia is the best tool for the job, in my opinion.

Wait, that's not all of them!?

That's right. There are still other tools you could use for screen recording. There are technically dozens of other options out there. While I could expound on a bunch more—Snagit, Quicktime, Open Broadcaster Software (OBS), ScreenRec, Nimbus Capture, CamStudio, ScreenFlow, Screenity, screencasting in Powtoon, Microsoft options (in Stream, PowerPoint, and Windows 10)—I'll spare you from whatever weird taco or blender-related tangents my mind might take you on in that process.

The most important thing to keep in mind here is that there's no one "right" tool, but there might be one that's "right" for you or your students. If you identify all of the characteristics of your situation and what you hope to achieve with screencasting, it'll likely become clear which one is best for you!

DECISION TIME!

Are you going to try out one of these tools? ☐ Yes ☐ No

Which one(s)?

☐ Screencastify   ☐ WeVideo
☐ Screencast-O-Matic   ☐ RecordCast
☐ Loom   ☐ Camtasia
☐ Flipgrid   ☐ Something else:_____

When are you going to try it out?

☐ Do Now   ☐ Do Soon   ☐ Do Later

Is there a certain lesson, activity, topic, or unit you'll use it for?

_____

_____

If it might solve a problem or meet one of your goals, it's worth committing to trying it out!

Don't forget to check out the resources and tutorials at the Online Resource Hub! There's probably a video about using the tool that you've selected!

(EduDuctTape.com/hub/chapter07)

SMART BOARDS, CRYING GRAPES, AND DOING BETTER

I walked into the kitchen one late afternoon to find my daughter, in tears, sobbing, and my wife, in tears, laughing. It was quite a spectacle. My daughter looked pretty clearly heartbroken; my wife looked like she just witnessed the funniest thing that she'd ever seen. It seems like an odd choice for a mom, who is also a school psychologist, to laugh at her crying child.

After they both calmed down, they had a talk about what had happened. My wife had been cleaning out my daughter's lunch box from that school day. She discovered that Parker had not eaten any of her grapes. She held up the baggie of grapes and asked Parker why she didn't eat them. She joked that the grapes were so sad that they hadn't been eaten. She asked Parker if she could hear the grapes crying. Parker, being our house softie, immediately started bawling. She felt horrible for the little grapes! She could imagine all of their sad faces. They had hoped to be eaten that day in the school cafeteria and their dreams . . . did not come true. Parker had left them in the baggie. Uneaten. Heartbroken.

After a short chat and some laughs, Parker understood that her mommy was joking and that, obviously, grapes did not have feelings. But, more importantly, she didn't need to feel bad about the fact that she no longer liked grapes and no longer wanted them in her lunch.

Sometimes we change our minds about things. Maybe it's because of new information or learning. Maybe it's because of a change of perspective or opinion. Maybe it's because we feel full after we eat our PBJ and just don't have room in our tummy for those grapes. But when we change, we don't need to feel bad about leaving old things behind. Especially if we are leaving them behind because we know better now.

About six years after I recorded the first video of myself doing the math homework on the SMART Board, I took on a new position as cocreator and teacher of my school's new STEM class. Our principal said, "I assume you want a SMART Board for your STEM classroom, right?"

Attempting to answer this question perplexed me. I had been using a SMART Board for seven years. More than a dozen educators who were preparing to use SMART Boards in their classes and multiple administrators who were considering purchasing SMART Boards had observed me in the classroom. A series of principals who all loved the things I was able to do in my classroom thanks to the SMART Board applauded me publicly and privately.

A SMART Board wasn't the right tool for the STEM course that I had in mind. I didn't feel like I should be at the front of a STEM classroom showing things on a SMART Board. I didn't believe I should be recording myself doing homework, much less assigning homework at all.

Actually, even if I was teaching math that year, I likely would not have used the SMART Board in the same way I had used it in the previous six years. My work on my district's recently formed technology leadership team had started to change my views of technology in the classroom. The ideas I found on Twitter had kicked my evolution into high gear. My participation in Twitter chats was a catalyst to a change in my mindset.

I started to realize that all of my uses of technology were just that: *my* uses of technology. And I suspected that a paraphrased version of the quote about "the one doing the talking is the one learning" was at play here: The one using the technology is the one learning.

The one using the technology is the one learning.

As my mindset had changed, so did my perspective, content, and curriculum. My beliefs about instruction, learning, and education constantly evolve. With new experiences and knowledge come new ways of thinking, teaching, and learning. A SMART Board was no longer the correct technology for me or my classroom. Screencasts of me doing math problems were no longer a fit for my curriculum or content, let alone my beliefs and knowledge.

I felt sad to give up my SMART Board along with some of the practices I had developed through the years. Like my daughter and her baggie full of grapes with imaginary emotions, I felt like I was letting someone down by changing. My SMART Board was my imagined crying inanimate object, albeit a less cute one than a tiny grape.

In retrospect, I realize it wasn't the SMART Board I felt sad about leaving behind. It wasn't even that I felt sad. I was worried.

I worried that changing my choice of technology and the way I had used edtech would mean I had been wrong before: that I was wrong to use a SMART Board, I was wrong to record myself going over homework, and I was wrong to play it for the whole class at the same time. I was concerned that if I stopped doing those things, everybody would know I had been wrong—that I was admitting failure.

Looking back, I know this is not an admission of error or failure. It's actually an admission of growth. An admission of reflecting, of changing perspectives, of taking new information into account, of revising beliefs.

So I told my principal that, no, I didn't want a SMART Board for my new classroom.

He was surprised, but after I explained my thoughts about how I felt my class should operate, and why a SMART Board was not a good fit, he understood. He didn't think I had been wrong before. He thought I was making an informed decision based on new information and new beliefs. He thought, I assume, I was open to new information and to looking at situations from an evolving perspective.

In one of my favorite quotes, Dr. Maya Angelou said "Do the best you can until you know better. Then when you know better, do better." Note that this famous quote isn't "Do the best you can until you realize you're wrong, and then when you realize that you're wrong, do what's correct." It's important for me to remember I wasn't *wrong* for using a SMART Board the way I did (and you're not wrong if you use it in that way, either). It's also important to remember I wasn't *bad* for that, either. Actually, I'm proud of what I was doing! I had identified specific problems—those transparency projector lessons, those eight minutes of math class—and came up with novel uses of technology to remedy those issues. Not only am I proud of what I did, I'm proud of the growth I exhibited as an educator!

> **"Do the best you can until you know better. Then when you know better, do better."**
> **—Dr. Maya Angelou**

Being proud of those strategies—or any strategy—doesn't mean I must remain committed to them forever. We can change our strategies or the technologies we use whenever we feel we *know better*. And, in doing so, it's not an admission that we previously *knew worse*. We were *doing the best we could*.

Humans find it difficult to change, I believe, not because of what we're changing to but because of what we're changing away from. It reminds me of a quote from Seth Godin: "The hard part isn't coming up with a new idea. The hard part is falling out of love with the old idea."

No one expects us, as educators or as humans, to be perfect. They just expect us to do the best we can. And, if *your best* is not as good as someone else's *best*, that's okay. It's okay to not be perfect. It's okay to not be as good as that teacher down the hall.

What's not okay? What's not okay is to *know better* and not *do better*. As you read this book, if something changes in your set of beliefs or your knowledge as an educator, you should take steps to *do better*. *When you know better, do better.*

When you observe a colleague, reflect on a lesson, attend a professional development, read an article online, or see a Tweet about a good teaching practice or technology tool, ask yourself, "Should I do things differently in my practice?" If the answer is *yes,* then you owe it to your students to take steps to do better. You don't have to do it all at once. But, *when you know better, do better.*

Start prioritizing those steps toward better. Then take the first one.

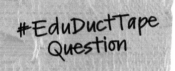

#EduDuctTape Question

How can I measure my students' understanding, not just their knowledge of the right or wrong answer?

Online Resource Hub—EduDuctTape.com/hub/chapter08

By the time I graduated from high school, I was probably six-foot-two-inches. I can remember the way opposing team members looked at me when I walked onto the basketball court as a high school basketball player. They had this, "Oh snap. I'm about to get dunked on" look on their faces. And then, they saw me dribble and shoot layups during warmups. Relief swept across their faces. They soon found out I was clumsy, awkward, and unable to jump more than a handful of inches off the floor.

The problem with judging a basketball player by height is that you're not measuring all aspects of the athlete. Just ask Tyrone "Muggsy" Bogues, who played fourteen seasons as an NBA point guard. Despite being the shortest player *ever* in the NBA at five-foot-three-inches, Bogues is the Charlotte Hornets' career leader in minutes played, assists, and steals. If you assessed his potential as a basketball player by looking only at his height, you'd fail to consider his forty-four-inch vertical jump, his speed, his defensive tenacity, his basketball acumen, and his superior passing ability.

We do the same things in our classrooms when we focus only on correct answers. While the tools we've discussed so far for assessing students have their place (certainly there is value in remembering vocabulary words and knowing the right answers), they're as effective in isolation as height is in comparing Muggsy Bogues and me as basketball players.

Although some tools can help us gather quick, actionable formative assessment data, we still need other tools to more deeply measure student comprehension and thinking. Using tools that allow us to see our students' understanding from different angles can help us more accurately assess our students and support them as learners. As educator and author Holly Clark puts it, "If we reexamine how we capture true knowledge and understanding from students, we have the ability to get inside every student's mind to figure out when they know something and when they don't."

Giving students an opportunity to articulate their thinking, verbalize their reasoning, and show their understanding is akin to watching Muggsy Bogues play a basketball game, rather than just looking at his height. Unfortunately, the same goes for watching me play a basketball game, rather than just looking at my height.

There's another reason to value other, more novel forms of assessment. They can be more fun, more engaging, and richer than the traditional strategies we are accustomed to. As National Board Certified teacher and author Rick Wormeli puts it, "Some educators treat assessment as an affliction rather than as a tool." Assessment strategies that bring in students' voice, creativity, and perspective can bring engagement, joy, and pride into the demonstration of learning while also giving teachers richer data and information about the students' understanding. To those who feel that moving from this *affliction* version of assessment to more novel alternatives lowers the bar of mastery, Wormeli points out, "To manipulate information . . ." to create the products involved in alternative assessments "requires mastery of the material."

> ## "Some educators treat assessment as an affliction rather than as a tool."
> **—Rick Wormeli**

Many educators and students experience a state of *flow* when creating products with the tools I'm about to share with you. In his book *Drive*, Daniel Pink describes Mihaly Csikszentmihalyi's idea of *flow* as experiences in which "people lived so deeply in the moment, and felt so utterly in control, that their sense of time, place and even self melted away." I'm confident all of your students can identify a flow-inducing tool in this list!

The strategies for using technology as a tool to help us measure students' understanding are nearly infinite and are limited only by the educators' and students' creativity. Let's look at a handful of options you could consider.

Decide: Is this #EduDuctTape question (on the previous page) one I need the answer to?

☐ **YES!** Continue below.   ☐ **NO!** Skim, if you'd like, then move on to the next chapter.

▶ **Think:** What would a rich assessment tool that's perfect **for me**, **my classroom**, **my students**, and **my content** look like? What does it need to do?

_____

_____

_____

TOOLS FOR VIDEO CREATION

Videos can be awesome assessment tools because they give us the ability to see representations of our students' thinking and hear their explanations of it simultaneously. Here are a few video creation tools your students could use for this.

Flipgrid

Every educational technology coach or leader knows to respond to a question including the words *video* and *response* with "Flipgrid." It's easy, it's free, and it's more than just plain video responses. Your students can:

✓ Use text or a "pen tool" in whiteboard mode, blackboard mode, or over an image.

✓ Use pictures (as *stickers*).

✓ Record screencasts.

✓ Edit, combine, or upload videos from other sources.

✓ Use greenscreen-like *Backdrops* or background-blurring to keep their surroundings more private.

✓ Add music to their recordings.

✓ Liven up their videos with filters and AR-style *Lenses*.

✓ ***Note:** a few of these features launch in Fall 2021.

And you can give your students video or text feedback and set it as public or private.

Flipgrid's features for collecting responses and giving feedback are better than any of the following options, but each one has features that merit mentioning. Plus, you always have the option of having your students use different tools and submit the products in Flipgrid!

Adobe Spark Video

Like the other two Adobe Spark tools (Post and Page), Adobe Spark Video makes the creation of visually appealing content slick and easy. There is a paid version of this tool available, but all of the necessary features are in the free version. You can combine pictures, video, text, icons, narration, and music.

- ✓ The easy-to-use slides-based (rather than timeline-based) editor makes video building simple.
- ✓ Transitions and effects are automatically added.
- ✓ You and your students can collaborate with others.

Screencastify Submit

As we discussed in Chapter 7, Screencastify Submit allows you to send a link out to your students, who then record webcam or screencast videos that automatically end up in your Google Drive. Your students will need to have Google accounts, but they do not need Screencastify accounts or the Screencastify extension. And, bonus, because the videos are in Google Drive, you can make comments on the video from within your Drive or, if you assign them as Google Classroom assignments, you can add comments and feedback there!

Green Screen by Do Ink

If you're an iOS user (iPad or iPhone), the inexpensive Do Ink app offers a kid-friendly quality video recording and editing program. Do Ink is known for its great green screen feature and masking feature (masking is kind of like manual green-screening). It is also a capable video editor that can work with images or videos taken from within the app or from your device's camera roll.

WeVideo

Want your students to create really impressive videos to demonstrate their understanding? Although Do Ink, Adobe Spark Video, and Flipgrid all offer video editing tools, WeVideo is the best web-based (not software) video editor out there. The free plan offers the editing basics, but the paid plans add in green screen tools, podcast creation, integration of Google Docs, and, most importantly, a classroom dashboard. Much like in Flipgrid and Screencastify Submit, you have the ability to assign, see, and assess student work without a tedious exporting and file sharing process.

Kapwing

This new tool, pronounced *ka-pwing* like "the sound of a bullet ricocheting off of metal," offers up lots of functionality for free in a web-based package. Your students can:

✓ Collaborate on projects.

✓ Add auto-generated and fully editable subtitles (captions) to their videos.

✓ Add text over their videos.

✓ Add animations to their videos.

✓ Add images to their videos.

✓ Crop their videos.

✓ Trim, split, and cut portions of their videos.

✓ Add audio to their videos.

✓ Create green screen videos or even use their tool to remove the background from videos not filmed in front of a green screen.

✓ Merge videos.

The crazy part of Kapwing is that all of this is available in the free version. The Pro version adds in some nice features, though:

★ Upload files up to 2 GB in size (up from 250 MB).

★ Export videos up to one hour long (up from seven minutes).

★ Unlimited video publishing (up from three hours of video per month).

★ Edit and store content for as long as needed (up from a two-day limit).

★ Make your content private.

That last bullet alludes to the major issue with Kapwing's services. In the terms of service, you are granting Kapwing a nonexclusive license to publish *your* (or *your students'*) videos, unless you are in the Pro version and make them private. With this disclaimer, it's probably not surprising that Kapwing is not intended for children under the age of thirteen.

If you can get past the privacy and terms of service limitations, you will certainly love what your students can do with Kapwing for free! And there are plenty of bonuses, including access to templates and the ability to create memes, GIFs, and images!

Prezi Video

I know what you're thinking: "No way, not Prezi. Those things give me vertigo!" I'm with you. The animations in Prezi slideshows were too intense, especially when in the hands of students. But I think you'll want to hear about the new addition to Prezi.

Like Flipgrid, Prezi Video is designed for making webcam videos. It adds in some slick overlays and animations, similar to the original Prezi—minus the vertigo. These animated overlays, which can include Prezi's visually appealing designs along with your own text and image content, are unlike anything you'll see in other video tools. Here are some of Prezi Video's current features:

- ✓ Transition freely between onscreen video overlays, webcam-only mode, or overlay-only mode (to focus on your content).
- ✓ Click through your overlays and contents just like a slideshow.
- ✓ Add text and images to your videos.
- ✓ Use Prezi's library of icons and templates.
- ✓ Import a PowerPoint to use in your video.
- ✓ Create videos up to fifteen minutes long.
- ✓ Present live in Zoom, Google Meet, and other platforms.
- ✓ Trim your video after recording.

The free version will let you or your students create some really cool videos, and the *Edu Plus* version adds in some nice features:

- ★ Unlimited video lengths
- ★ Full HD videos
- ★ Presenter notes
- ★ Video downloads, allowing you to post them elsewhere
- ★ Offline video recording
- ★ Prezi watermark removal

Wait, that's not all of them!?

If that's not enough options, you could look at the screencast tools like Screencastify, Screencast-O-Matic, and RecordCast that we discussed earlier, as well as tools like Explain Everything!

◼ TOOLS FOR AUDIO CREATION AND EDITING

While the ability to combine audio with visuals makes videos an assessment all-star, there are also times when audio is enough.

Soundtrap

Soundtrap for Education is probably the ideal tool here. It integrates with most learning management systems, allows you to create assignments from within Google

Classroom, gives you easy access to your students' recordings, and organizes the recordings by assignment. It's not free, but if this is a major facet of your assessment strategy, it may be worth the money.

SoundTrap is a great multitrack audio editor that will work on all kinds of devices. My favorite SoundTrap feature is the transcript-based editor in which spoken word is automatically turned into a transcript for easy editing. Want to edit out an "um"? Just find it in the transcript, highlight it, and delete it. Doing this deletes it from the audio too! As a nice accessibility feature, you can also copy that transcript's text and paste it elsewhere.

Other Multitrack Audio Recording and Editing Options

Multitrack means you can have multiple pieces of audio playing simultaneously or overlapping one another, such as music in one track and your voice in another. These tools might be a little challenging for younger learners, but once they learn to use them, just imagine what they could create!

If your students are using Apple or iOS devices, the answer should be obvious. **GarageBand** has been making music recording and audio editing attainable for non-audiophiles since way back in 2004. Although the pile of features and capabilities in GarageBand is high, the bar for learning to use it is relatively low. And if that's not enough of an endorsement: it's the program that I use for recording and editing the *Educational Duct Tape* podcast!

If you're up for using a multitrack audio editor that a podcaster would use, the most common in the podcast industry is **Audacity**. This widely used, open-source audio recording and editing program is free, relatively easy to learn, and works on both Mac and Windows.

If you're already using **WeVideo** in the classroom, you may want to use it for audio projects as well! While the editor will look like their regular video editor, the ability to record and edit multiple tracks of audio is nice. Add in their collection of commercially licensed, royalty-free stock audio, and you've got a great option. Once recording is done, the audio files can be hosted on WeVideo for easy sharing, downloaded as an MP3, or easily sent to Drive, DropBox, or OneDrive.

Twisted Wave is free and browser-based, but also offers a paid iOS app and Mac software. On the online version, free accounts are capped to five-minute audio files, and files are only stored online for thirty days. After editing the audio, it can be downloaded in a variety of file formats or sent to Google Drive or SoundCloud.

Beautiful Audio Editor can be accessed from within Google Drive. Your projects can be saved to Google Drive or your hard drive. When you're all done, you can download your files as MP3 or .wav files.

Simple Recording Tools

Want a super-simple recording option? This next set of options only have a single track, and most do not offer any editing options. However, giving up those features means you gain simplicity.

Screencastify's *export as an audio file* option is a step below the multitrack editors above, but a step above the other simple recording options we'll discuss, because you are able to cut and trim your audio and merge in other recordings before exporting it. Just record as if you were doing a screencast, edit as needed, and then export the recording as an audio file. The free version limits you to five-minute recordings, though.

Vocaroo is a web-based recorder that allows users to record, share, and download. There are no editing features to learn! Because recordings are hosted on the Vocaroo site, they can be linked into other locations or embedded on other sites. Unfortunately, though, Vocaroo doesn't guarantee your recordings will stay on the site for more than a few months.

Mote is a Chrome extension that was initially used for adding audio comments into Google Docs, Slides, Sheets, and Classroom. Mote later added in the ability to record from anywhere in Chrome, share *Sticky Motes,* which link recordings to specific websites, and even to add audio directly into Google Slides, Google Forms, and Gmail. On top of all of that, Mote added an iOS app that allows you to record from anywhere on your iPhone or iPad. Those recordings are accessible from other devices where you're logged into your account. The free version allows recordings up to thirty seconds in length. In the paid versions, you can increase the recording length and even have Mote create transcripts of your audio.

Flipgrid (*seriously, Jake, Flipgrid again?*) also allows audio-only responses to topics! You wouldn't be able to use them as audio files elsewhere (without some crafty file converting), but housing these responses in their great platform might be a huge win for you!

AudioVoiceRecorder.com is a web-based option that will allow you to quickly record from any browser and download your audio as an MP3 file.

Cloud Audio Recorder is a website-based recorder that allows users to export files as MP3 files or .wav files (wavs are higher quality, but also larger files) and either download them or send them directly to Google Drive. One thing I do not like about this site is the number and type of advertisements on it.

▨ TOOLS FOR ANIMATION

Creating animations is a great way to combine visuals and audio while giving learners the opportunity to tap into their creativity. The issue here is that creating animations is often more time consuming than recording a video or audio response.

Animation and Drawing by Do Ink

This may be the best animation option available for classrooms, but, unfortunately, it's currently only available on iPads. Animations can include text, photos, available props, or user-created drawings. Objects can be easily animated using the *pathing* tool to select the path that an object will follow, as well as its size and shape, during the animation. For Green Screen by Do Ink app users, the multitrack animation editor will be familiar because it is much like the timeline editor in that app. Although the app doesn't have the ability to include audio, you could easily add it by screen recording or exporting the animation to a video-creation tool. If you and your students have access to iPads, check out this inexpensive app!

Scratch

This Massachusetts Institute of Technology (MIT) Media Lab creation often gets pegged as a great tool for learning about computer science and programming. Although that is accurate, it's also a fantastic tool for creating animations. On my fortieth birthday, my daughter, who was eight at the time, created a "Happy Birthday" animation in Scratch on our Chromebook, and my six-year-old son created an animation on the simplified iOS app ScratchJr. If they can pull that off, then they obviously could have created animations for academic content that would have blown their teachers' socks off.

For the most part, your students' creativity and willingness to learn are the only limitations to Scratch's capabilities. They can add audio, images, text, speech bubbles, characters, and their own drawings. If you explore the published projects at scratch.mit.edu, you'll find a wide variety of formats, including music videos, animations, and interactive games. Scratch is available for free (as is the iOS or Android ScratchJr app) and although there are learning resources available from Google CS First and other sources, the best way to learn to use it is to try it out!

#StopMotionSlides

Creating stop motion animations with Google Slides is one of my favorite activities to do and one of my favorite professional development sessions to lead. This process, which could be replicated on Microsoft PowerPoint or Apple Keynote, puts me in a total state of flow.

The process of creating stop motion animations with a slideshow tool is much like the flip books you may have created as a young'un. Each slide is an incremental change from the previous slide. When you scroll through the slides, those incremental changes give the appearance of movement.

Here is the general process for creating #StopMotionSlides:

1. Make a plan! It can be tedious to go back and make changes, so it helps to have a plan in mind from the very beginning.
2. Set up your first slide. Include objects, backgrounds, text, and shapes as you wish.
3. Create a copy of that first slide.
4. On that new slide (slide #2) move objects to make an incremental change.
5. Create a copy of that second slide.
6. On *that* new slide (slide #3), move objects again to make another incremental change.
7. Repeat this process until your entire animation is complete!

You can see more extensive tips about this process in the Online Resource Hub!

Flipgrid

Is he really coming back to Flipgrid again!? Yup! Flipgrid has a collection of stickers that can be dragged around the screen to create animation-like videos. Your students can even use their own pictures!

Your students can create stop motion animations in Flipgrid by recording their video in one-second segments. Set the scene, press record, press pause, make a change, press record, press pause, rinse, repeat, creativity!

TOOLS TO CREATE VISUALS

"If you can't explain it simply, you don't understand it well enough." This quote, typically credited to Albert Einstein (though likely erroneously), perfectly sums up why creating simple visual representations of understanding may be a perfect assessment tool. If a student can demonstrate comprehension of a concept in a simple, visually appealing graphic, they likely have a firm grasp of it (and also have a knack for a skill that is valuable in our society).

Canva

You may have already used Canva to create a flyer, Christmas card, infographic, or other graphic. If you have, you've probably experienced the frustration of needing to pay for that perfect icon, image, or design. But with Canva for Education, you don't have to spend a dime. It's free! You have access to some awesome features:

- ✓ An insanely large number of templates
- ✓ Plenty of fonts
- ✓ Free-to-use stock photos, videos, and graphics
- ✓ Shapes, text, icons, GIFs, videos, audio, and emojis
- ✓ A charts option that lets students add bar graphs, line graphs, area graphs, pie charts, and donut charts to their projects
- ✓ An option to add content from third-party apps, including YouTube, Bitmoji, Google Drive, Giphy, Google Maps, and more

But it's not just the creation that you'll benefit from in Canva for Education:

- ✓ Create assignments.
- ✓ Create class groups.
- ✓ View student work.
- ✓ Comment on student work.

Adobe Spark

If your goal is the easy creation of awesome, visually appealing graphics and pages, Adobe Spark also deserves mention here. We discussed one of the three facets of Adobe Spark—*Video*—earlier, but *Post* and *Page* are great tools for creating visuals in the classroom. Like Canva, Adobe offers its premium features to educators and students for free. That means your students can show their understanding with responsive web pages with *Adobe Spark Page* and visually appealing graphics with *Adobe Spark Post*. You and your students can do some cool things:

- ✓ Use templates.
- ✓ Add music and photos.

✓ Use a variety of fonts.

Their creations may rival those made in Canva, but Adobe Spark's offerings fall short of what Canva provides in terms of classroom functionality (assignments, comments, collaboration, and more).

Wait, that's not all of them!?

There are tons of tools that you and your students can use for creating visuals. Venngage, for example, is great for data visualization and infographics, but falls short of what Canva offers for free. Similarly, Piktochart is great for creating charts from dynamic or imported data and turning graphics into presentations, but it also has a price tag. If you're worried about the dolla dolla bills, but Canva and Adobe Spark don't meet your needs, you can also turn to tools that are freely available in your regular tech ecosystem, such as Slides or Drawings for the Google folks and PowerPoint or Sway for the Microsoft peeps.

THE SWISS ARMY KNIFE TOOLS

Video, animations, audio, and visuals are all great options for getting an accurate depiction of your students' comprehension, but what if you want to empower your students with the choice of how to demonstrate their learning? You could say "Use *this* or *this* or *this*," but what if you want them all to use the same tool, yet have some choice in what kind of representation to make? Let's talk about a few tools that do this.

Book Creator

When the original iPhone came out, it was only available on AT&T. I was a Verizon user and I was so jealous of my iPhone-using AT&T friends. I had the same experience with Book Creator. For its first few years of existence, it was an iPads-only app. As a teacher in a Windows and Chromebook school, I was super "jelly" of teachers whose students were creating awesome ebooks on their iPads.

But, just like the day the iPhone came to Verizon, I jumped at the opportunity to use Book Creator as soon as it hit Chromebooks. My first impression? *Wow, you can do a lot with this tool!*

✓ Add text, images, videos, and audio files.

✓ Embed Google Maps.

✓ Embed just about anything off the web.

✓ Record audio.

✓ Take webcam pictures.

✓ Record webcam videos.

✓ Create drawings.

✓ Create AutoDraw drawings.

Although its best feature—collaboration—is part of the paid version, your students can show their thinking in a plethora of ways within the free version!

Padlet

Padlet is one of the ultimate Swiss Army knives in all of edtech. Although some people are put off by the limitations on their free plan—most users can only create three "walls"—your students can still show their thinking in a variety of ways on the free version:

✓ Add text, links, videos, images, and GIFs.

✓ Take webcam pictures.

✓ Record webcam videos.

✓ Record audio.

✓ Screen record.

✓ Create drawings.

Plus, with their variety of layouts—*wall, canvas, stream, grid,* and *shelf*—their projects will look cool, too. Add in the other two layouts—*maps* and *timeline*—and you've got a tool that lives up to its price tag.

Seesaw

Every time I talk to educators about Seesaw, I have to tell them, "It's not just for elementary classrooms!" While it's an easy-to-use tool for "littles," students of any age can leverage the high-powered options for personal expression. This learning management system, digital portfolio, and parent communication hybrid tool makes so much possible!

✓ Add webcam images.

✓ Add drawings.

✓ Annotate images (within the drawing tool).

✓ Record videos.

✓ Create notes.

✓ Record audio (within the photo, drawing, or note tools).

✓ Add links.

✓ Upload files.

So . . . pretty much anything.

Take that "anything is possible" and multiply it by two because students are also *empowered* to add, create, and post artifacts of learning whenever they want. The only downside of this tool is you probably wouldn't want to use it for one-off activities. It would be an awesome tool to use across an entire school year, but it might be too much for a single project.

Genially

Genially is a pretty new tool on the edtech scene. Students can use this visual story-creation platform to make presentations, infographics, gamification experiences, interactive images, video presentations, and more. These interactive creations can have multiple pages and include text, images, GIFs, videos, audio, tables, pop-up windows, maps, surveys, PDFs, Google Forms, and more. There's also a handy feature for adding passwords to pages, which is nice for privacy, but also handy for making activities like breakouts! As if all of that weren't enough, it includes a plethora of awesome templates for infographics, maps, quizzes, gamifications, timelines, presentations, and more! While some of the templates and other features are part of the premium plans, your students will be able to do plenty in the free version to model their comprehension. And they can collaborate on their creations too!

Google Slides or Microsoft PowerPoint

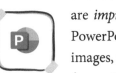

Remember when I told you being impressive is not the goal, being effective is? Well, this is a good time to remind you of that truth. Book Creator, Padlet, and Seesaw are *impressive* tools, but tried-and-true options like Google Slides and Microsoft PowerPoint are *effective* ones, too. Your learners can easily add text, drawings, images, webcam pictures, videos, audio files, charts, and diagrams into both platforms. Empowering your students to use some of those features to give you a peek into their brains? That's *effective* and *impressive*.

Wait, that's not all of them!?

There's a reason that Home Depot and Lowe's stores are the size of airplane hangars. There are so many tools! The same is true with educational technology, and the Swiss Army knife tools are no exception. Your learners could demonstrate their knowledge in multiple ways with Wakelet,

Webjets, Microsoft OneNote, Microsoft Sway, and a handful of other tools. But you don't need *all* of the tools. You just need the one(s) that work for you and your students.

DECISION TIME!

Are you going to try out one of these tools?   ☐ Yes   ☐ No

Which one(s)?

☐ Flipgrid	☐ Cloud Audio Recorder
☐ Adobe Spark Video	☐ Animations and Drawings by Do Ink
☐ Screencastify Submit	☐ Scratch
☐ Green Screen by Do Ink	☐ #StopMotionSlides
☐ WeVideo	☐ Canva
☐ Kapwing	☐ Adobe Spark
☐ GarageBand	☐ Venngage
☐ Audacity	☐ Piktochart
☐ WeVideo for audio	☐ Book Creator
☐ Twisted Wave	☐ Padlet
☐ Beautiful Audio Editor	☐ Seesaw
☐ Screencastify for audio	☐ Genially
☐ Vocaroo	☐ Google Slides
☐ Flipgrid for audio	☐ Microsoft PowerPoint
☐ Mote	☐ Something else:_____
☐ AudioVoiceRecorder.com	

When are you going to try it out?

☐ Do Now   ☐ Do Soon   ☐ Do Later

Is there a certain lesson, activity, topic, or unit you'll use it for?

_____

_____

If it might solve a problem or meet one of your goals, it's worth committing to trying it out!

Don't forget to check out the resources and tutorials at the Online Resource Hub! There's probably a video about using the tool that you've selected!

EduDuctTape.com/hub/chapter08

NINE

MISBEHAVING STUDENTS, HONEST REFLECTIONS, AND AN EQUATION

Jake Miller
October 4, 2013 at 10:43 AM · 👥

Sometimes, during my 2nd period class, I legitimately consider curling up on the floor, closing my eyes, and rocking myself.

👍 Like   💬 Comment   ↪ Share

That's an actual Facebook post of mine. It's not fabricated. I was in the middle of a nine-week grading period with the most challenging class I have ever taught. It was one of the first groups in that eighth-grade STEM class I mentioned in the previous chapter. Every kid in our middle school took STEM for a quarter of the school year as part of their exploratory class rotation. This particular class made me wonder,

- "What was in the water thirteen years ago?"
- "Was I mean to one of the guidance counselors at the staff party?"
- "How did this group of students end up together?"
- "Am I on some kind of reality TV show? Is Ashton Kutcher 'punking' me?"

As you can see from the Facebook post, I was not taking much ownership over this problem. It was something that was happening *to* me. I was just an innocent party in this difficult class. Or so I thought.

If you were to look at the responses to the post, you'd see similar patterns in the responses of my colleagues.

- "Dude, I've seen who is in that class period. That's a rough group!"

- "You're telling me! I have most of those same students in my fourth period class!"
- "For sure! I had to cover for you last week. Good luck getting that class to learn."

Not only did I need to remedy this situation to remedy my increasingly frequent headaches, but I also needed to remedy it to adhere to our buddy John Hattie's insights. As Hattie's 2018 data showed, the effect size of *decreasing disruptive behavior* was 0.34, placing it in the "likely to have positive impact on student achievement" tier.

At some point after I made that post, I reflected on what was happening in this class. I went through the thirty-ish students who were in the room and made a list of the kids who presented behavior problems. As I made that list, I started realizing the students fit in two categories:

Students who were highly capable or fast processors who were goofing off while they waited for my instructional pace to catch up with them.

Students who were slower processors or lower-ability-level students who were unable to keep up with my pace.

What about all of my "Goldilocks students"? The ones the porridge is just right for? They were behaving well. It was at this moment I realized that not only was I part of the cause of my struggles, but I could potentially be a part of the solution.

You see, as I truly reflected on the situation, I realized there were some things over which I had no control: the group of students in that class, their ability levels, the pace at which they learned, their motivation, and their behavior choices. I had a desired outcome: all students on-task, well-behaved, happy, engaged, empowered, proud, and learning. If I hoped to get the outcome I wanted, I would need to choose the right response to the factors I couldn't dictate. My response was the way I could control—or at least intentionally influence—the outcome. My realizations helped me see I could respond with a change that might steer the situation toward the outcome I wanted. So I did. And it worked.

We'll discuss my solution in the #EduDuctTape Question for this chapter, but first, I'd like to share my favorite equation with you. And no, it's not the quadratic equation or the theory of relativity.

$$E \quad + \quad R \quad = \quad O$$

| The Event | Your Response | The Outcome |

The Success Principles author and motivational speaker Jack Canfield made this a well-known equation. While I don't believe that the equation is applicable in all situations (not all events are created equally and not all desired outcomes are realistic), I think it's a very useful lens for thinking about technology integration and other classroom practices.

If we focus on the **Events** (our students, their learning styles, our available technology, our curriculum, etc.) and identify our goals—or, in this equation, our desired **Outcome**—then we can focus on identifying a **Response** that can steer us to that outcome.

In my situation, I needed to identify a response that could lead me on the path to my outcome.

How can I create a student-paced learning environment?

Online Resource Hub—EduDuctTape.com/hub/chapter09

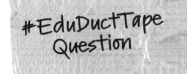
#EduDuctTape Question

TOOLS FOR STUDENT-PACED LEARNING

Once I realized organizing my class around a standardized pace of instruction was a major catalyst of the behavior problems in my classroom, I knew what type of change I needed to make. I needed to allow for differentiation in the pace at which my students moved through the content. I needed to put my students in the driver's seat. So I created a student-paced course.

Decide: Is this #EduDuctTape question (above) one I need the answer to?

☐ **YES!** Continue below.   ☐ **NO!** Skim, if you'd like, then move on to the next chapter.

▶ **Think**: What would a student-paced course that's perfect **for me, my classroom, my students,** and **my content** look like? What does it need to do?

_____

_____

_____

_____

Google Sites

I knew my Google Apps for Education account gave me access to a free website maker (Google Sites), where I could list all of my activities and assignments in order and have them link to Google Docs, Google Slides, YouTube videos, and other web-based resources. So I created a website. Then, my students simply needed to go through the activities and assignments in order.

Activity/Assignment List:		
Activity/Assignment:	**Details, Steps, Links:**	**Objectives:** _(why we're doing the activity)_
1. Icebreaker Activity	Done as a group in class.	- _To learn about our classmates._ - _To experience collaborating on a Google Presentation._
2. Welcome Letter	Read over with parent/guardian, sign bottom, cut off & return.	- _To understand the rules and expectations of STEM8 Class._
3. Power Tower Activity #1	We will do this one all together!	- _To experience the Engineering Design Process._ - _To apply our knowledge of gravity, air resistance, friction and other science topics._
4. Power Tower Activity #2	We will do this one all together! **At least one member of your group needs to take a video**	- _Developing & utilizing rules for good teamwork._ - _To experience the Engineering Design Process._ - _To apply our knowledge of gravity, air resistance, friction and other science topics._
5. Answer Universal Vocab Questions #1-2	Open the "Universal Vocab Questions" document in your STEM Assignment Folder and answer questions #1-2	- _Showing what we learned from recent activities._
6. STEM Careers Project Part 1	Visit the website and use it to select a STEM Career that you're interested in researching. When you've selected one, click on the link on the page to tell me what career you'll be researching. Then . . . go back to this assignment in Classroom and **Mark as Done.**	- _Learning about STEM Careers._ - _Selecting a STEM Career to research._

Now, I don't want you to think this was a flawless integration from Day One. My eighth-grade students had gone through years of instruction that, for the most part, was not student-paced. This was an adjustment for them. On many occasions students would ask me things like, "Mr. Miller, I just finished Activity 2. What should I do now?"

I would say, predictably, "Activity 3."

As my students assimilated to this new format, however, I found that it was solving my problem. It was an **R** that was responding to my **E** in a way that got me closer to my **O**. The behavior problems in my classroom drastically reduced. It didn't solve all of them—this is a middle school, not a utopia—but it was effective.

What I discovered, as we often find with technology integrations, was that this use of Google Sites along with Docs, Slides, and YouTube videos actually achieved goals I didn't realize I had! My students took more ownership over their learning and success! Removing myself from the front of the classroom gave me the opportunity to converse with students and help deepen their understanding, enrich their experience, and assess their growth. The website didn't solve all of the behavior problems, but it granted me more freedom to focus on students who were still struggling or misbehaving.

I remember one day, a few days after making this change, I was standing in the hallway between classes, chatting with a coworker. After the bell rang, I took a deep breath, mentally prepared myself for getting all of the students quiet, and walked back into my classroom. But instead of seeing a classroom full of students who had mysteriously not heard the bell, I discovered a totally new phenomenon. Most of the students were not talking. They were not up and wandering around the room. They were *working*. It turns out they weren't waiting for me to start class. They were waiting for something to do. They were waiting to be given responsibility. A student-paced course put them in the driver's seat. And many of them were ready to hit the gas pedal.

Again, though, it wasn't perfect. Some students still needed some prodding or coaxing. Technology can enhance and even revolutionize the classroom, but not without a good teacher. And the great news, in this situation, was that with 90 percent of my students on task at their own pace, I could prod, coax, or support the other 10 percent without slowing everyone else down.

One interesting thing about using an *Educational Duct Tape* mindset and an E + R = O mindset in your classroom is that addressing one goal or solving one problem often helps you identify other problems or goals. And each of these steps helps you improve the student learning experience more and more. In upcoming chapters, we'll hear about the *other* problems and goals I confronted in this class.

■ OTHER STRATEGIES

If I were developing this course today, I might still choose to use Google Sites, but I'd also give some serious consideration to some tools that have come out or vastly improved in recent years. What should *you* use? Well, it is up to *you*! You should pick the option that best fits you, your content, and your students. Here are some options you may want to consider!

Google Classroom

If you teach at a Google school, this is the most obvious choice. Google Classroom is designed to be used in a teacher-paced format, but many teachers have had success in using it for student-paced courses as well.

The major downside of using Google Classroom for this is that the setup might make it difficult for your students to ignore *future* assignments and focus on *current* assignments. You can try three things to remedy this:

- ✓ Turn off the setting that posts new assignments on the Stream.
- ✓ Instruct your students to turn off notifications for new assignments.
- ✓ Only assign things to students who are ready (or nearly ready) for them.

Microsoft Teams

Like Classroom, Microsoft Teams is also a highly capable classroom management platform you could use in student-paced settings for a handful of reasons:

- ✓ Access to all Office 365 tools (Word, Excel, PowerPoint, and others)
- ✓ An ecosystem of educational applications
- ✓ Integration of Microsoft Forms

Wakelet

I think this might be my front-runner choice if I had to make a student-paced course from scratch. With Wakelet, you can:

- ✓ Add any kind of content.
- ✓ Rearrange content by dragging and dropping.
- ✓ Use images and text to break up units or assignments.
- ✓ Easily add video with Flipgrid Shorts.

✓ Set your *collections* and *spaces* (multiple collections combined together) as private, public, or unlisted.

✓ Organize your *collections* and *spaces* as you see fit.

✓ Collaborate with other Wakelet-using educators.

✓ Add text, YouTube videos, tweets, images, PDFs, Google Drive files, Microsoft OneDrive files, and, as I mentioned above, videos created with Flipgrid Shorts.

✓ Add anything else on the web, using URLs (web addresses).

The biggest reason I'd use Wakelet for this is the ease of adding video. When "2012 Jake" wanted to add video instructions to his student-paced course, he had to record them in the PC version of Screencast-O-Matic, upload them to YouTube, and then link them to his site. In Wakelet, just click the Flipgrid Shorts button and you can record quick webcam videos or screencasts, or even edit together multiple clips!

ⓢ Schoology

How do you pronounce that? *Skoo-awloe-gee?*

When I entered my role as a Technology Integration Specialist, the school had already opted to use Schoology (*it's pronounced school-oh-gee*) as its learning management system, gradebook, and location where parents accessed student grades and assignments. Saying I was not excited is an understatement. Listening to parents attempt to pronounce *Schoology* did not help. After three years of using the platform, I fell in love with some of the features that could be great for student-paced courses. You can use it for several things:

✓ Build out courses or units.

✓ Utilize a robust materials and assignments organization system.

✓ Use their built-in assessments.

✓ Use their built-in gradebook.

✓ Organize assignments, materials, links, and resources into folders.

✓ Set *Student Completion Rules.*

That last one was the big one for me. Let's say that you build a unit with six elements. With *Completion Rules,* you can set it so that your students have to take the pre-assessment before watching the video, have to watch the video before accessing an article, and so on. The real beauty is that you can also set specific *Completion Rules;* for example, it could be set that your students have to *submit* a Google Doc in an assignment before moving on to the discussion board and *post a comment* in the discussion board before taking the summative assessment. The best function of all is that you can require your students to score above a certain percentage on that summative assessment before moving on to the next item. That feature is perfect if you have a mastery-based classroom. You can also nest these activities into folders and then set *Completion Rules* on the folders themselves, requiring students to complete one entire set of activities before moving on to another.

For a student-paced course, those features are good enough to change its name to "School O.G." *(Get it?)*

Eduflow

The best kind of student-paced learning experience is one that *flows*. This option is so focused on building that *flow*, that they put it in their name.

Eduflow started out as Peergrade, which I loved for doing peer reviews. What made Peergrade great was the *flow* of the peer reviews. Students were led through submitting their work, anonymously reviewing peers, viewing their own feedback, and, finally, reflecting on their feedback. With that streamlined, pedagogically sound process, it's not surprising the team behind Peergrade saw its potential for educational experiences that didn't involve peer feedback. Eduflow came out of that realization, and it could be powerful for student-paced coursework. Before I get into the *flow* of this description, I need to point out that Eduflow's free version limits you to fifteen students per thirty-day window and a total of 3 GB of storage.

✓ Create courses, units, mini-units, and lessons that your students go through in order.

✓ Include your own content or curated content in your activities:

  ▶ Add text, images, videos, and file uploads into activity content.

  ▶ Use the built-in webcam and screen recording tools to add content.

✓ Select from a variety of tasks for your students:

  ▶ Assignment submissions (can include Google Drive files, uploaded files, text, or links)

  ▶ Peer review

  ▶ Feedback reflection

  ▶ Self-review

✓ Set prerequisites and deadlines for activities.

✓ Develop differentiated personalized learning paths for your students.

✓ Use Eduflow's pre-built flows.

And the best part is that you can see your students' progress as they *flow* through the course! (*Did I say "flow" enough times in this section!?*)

Other Website Tools

If you like the idea of my Google Site but have something against Google Sites or don't have a Google account, why not use a different website maker for this activity? You could use a Wix, Weebly, WordPress, or any other site builder out on the market! Just make sure it has satisfactory privacy settings and user agreements for your school or district.

Seesaw

Seesaw is like Google Classroom mixed with a digital portfolio with a dash of Remind (a teacher–parent and teacher–student communication tool). Just like in Google Classroom, you could certainly post a series of activities and assignments for your students to complete. A few additional features make it a great option for student-paced learning:

✓ You can create materials, resources, and instructions for your activities within Seesaw.

✓ You can record a video or voice instructions within the assignment.

✓ Your students can curate work they're proud of as they go, empowering them and thrilling their parents!

Just like Google Classroom, the downside here is this format may be overwhelming for your students because they'll see activities pop up when they're posted, rather than just seeing them at the bottom of the list like they were on my website. Like in Classroom, however, you could only assign activities to the students who are ready for them and then add other students when they catch up.

Google Docs or Microsoft Word

I said earlier that what is important is how we teach with the technology, not the technology we teach with. I also said, you don't need an observer to be wowed by the technology you are using; you need the observer to be wowed by how you are using the technology.

I can tell you from experience: a student-paced tech course *wows* people. If that's your goal, you don't necessarily need a new piece of technology to do so. Can we do this with Google Docs or Microsoft Word? Let's see . . .

What kind of things does a student-paced course need?

✓ A numbered list of activities. *Check.*

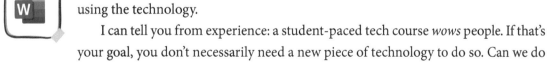

✓ Links to resources. *Check.*

✓ A link students can access? *Check.*

Create the doc, share it as *can view*, and add to it throughout the year! If fancy is important to you, you could build your course in that no-frills Google Doc in year one and then transition it to a website in year two!

Google Slides or Microsoft PowerPoint

Want to go with something comfortable and familiar but with a little more design aesthetic than a word processor? Why not Google Slides or PowerPoint? The beauty here is that not only can you add text and links, but you can also embed videos and other resources right into the slides. In this format, instead of a long document with numbered activities, each slide can be a different activity. That means you can see at a glance which slide each student is on!

Google Sheets or Microsoft Excel

A spreadsheet fanatic like me can't possibly write this list and not give a hat tip to a spreadsheet option here. It may not look as pretty *to you* (I think they're beautiful!) as some of the other options, but spreadsheets are masters of ordered lists. And you could even kick that beauty up a notch with some checkboxes for each student to check off as they complete each activity.

Wait, that's not all of them!?

That's right; it's about pedagogy, not the tool. And, therefore, there are a plethora of other tools I could add here. One of my graduate school professors would be irritated if I didn't mention Moodle (*as would some guy on Twitter who Tweet-scolded me the other day for showing how to do something in Google Sheets rather than in Moodle*). Their fanatical obsession with Moodle aside, they'd both be correct: it *would* work great here. So would other learning management systems such as Canvas, Blackboard, and Edmodo.

While we're at it, tools like Padlet, Genially, Trello, Basecamp, and probably dozens more would work great as well! And there are even ways you could get creative with other edtech tools such as Flipgrid and Google My Maps to build student-paced courses.

DECISION TIME!

Are you going to try out one of these tools? ☐ Yes ☐ No

Which one(s)?

- ☐ Google Sites
- ☐ Google Classroom
- ☐ Microsoft Teams
- ☐ Wakelet
- ☐ Schoology
- ☐ Another Website Tool:_____

- ☐ Seesaw
- ☐ Docs or Word
- ☐ Slides or PowerPoint
- ☐ Sheets or Excel
- ☐ Something else:_____

When are you going to try it out?

☐ Do Now ☐ Do Soon ☐ Do Later

Is there a certain lesson, activity, topic, or unit you'll use it for?

_____

_____

If it might solve a problem or meet one of your goals, it's worth committing to trying it out!

Don't forget to check out the resources and tutorials at the Online Resource Hub! There's probably a video about using the tool that you've selected!

EduDuctTape.com/hub/chapter09

CLASSROOM WALKS, QUIET STUDENTS, AND DR. ANGELOU AGAIN

Back in Chapter 9, I shared the way I used a Google Site to turn my teacher-led class into a student-paced course. My original problem, as you may recall, was that keeping all students on the same pace was causing behavior problems. So, I used Google Sites along with YouTube, Screencast-O-Matic, Google Docs, and Google Slides to create a web-based course that my students could move through at their own pace.

In one of the last sentences of that chapter, I pointed out that, even though this had solved that problem, it wasn't perfect. Sometimes, solving one problem or addressing one goal exposes the next problem or goal so that we can see it. That was the case with my STEM class.

After I made the transition to a student-paced course, what I did during a class period changed drastically. Instead of leading the class from the front of the room, I transitioned to moving around the room. I would start at one side of the room and walk, row-by-row, through my classroom.

I really enjoyed circulating through my classroom in this fashion. It wasn't my glee about "getting my steps in" that made me like this; it was the discussion I was having with my students. Initially, I thought I'd use this time to help keep students on task and to answer questions as needed. I found I also used much of this time to *ask* questions. I discovered that, when using traditional direct instruction, opportunities to ask questions of a higher order and hear from our students are pretty rare. In my new format, I could ask every student a higher-order question without detracting from the pace of the other students. I treasured these exciting conversations and the deepened and shared learning outcomes.

A new problem presented itself later in the class period. One day, after chatting with, helping, or redirecting the first twenty-five kids in my classroom walk, I came to the last student in the room. By this time, only a few minutes remained in class. This student—let's call her Anita—was staring at the blinking cursor on her computer screen. I asked her, "Anita, why aren't you doing anything?"

She responded, "I don't understand this activity."

As a rational adult, it's probably obvious to you that Anita should have raised her hand and asked me for help. But she didn't. Behaviors like this are typical with middle schoolers. We know that the rational thing is to ask for help, but we also know that expecting middle schoolers to always do the rational thing is, well, irrational.

This happened more than once, and it wasn't always Anita in this situation. Sometimes, the students would be closer to the beginning of my classroom walk, so they lost less of our valuable class time while they waited for me to discover their need for help—but they still lost time. As we discussed back in Chapter 9, I can't control the Event, but I could focus on selecting a **Response** that would help me get to my desired **Outcome**.

Let's review our situation here:

- **Event:** Some students are not willing to raise their hand to express confusion or ask for help when they need it.
- **Ideal Outcome:** All students are able to maximize their time in my classroom and receive the help and support that they need as soon as possible.
- **Response** . . .

My response was to add a Google Form to the top of my Google Site. Before I get to what the Google Form asked, or how it helped me, let's talk about the things I was aware of:

- I had observed and reflected on the Event and the circumstances.
- I was knowledgeable about what I could do with a Google Form.
- I was aware I could view the results of a Google Form in Google Sheets.
- I was aware it was possible to embed a Google Form in a Google Site. (Embedded means it's shown in the site, not simply hyperlinked on the site.)

Based on my knowledge and my observations, I felt confident that this could help me with this problem. I added the Form. It had four questions:

- What's your name?
- What class period is it?
- What activity are you on?
- Is there anything else that you need to tell me?

Home

Please follow through the class content in order. Make sure that you've completed and submitted all portions of the activity or assignments prior to moving on to the following activity or assignment. *When it comes to partner or group work, you are allowed to temporarily skip one activity or assignment so that you can work with a group as long as you then return to the correct step.*

Always fill out this form before starting your work for the day!

What Activity # are you on?

We fill this out at the BEGINNING of each class period so that Mr. Miller knows what activity you're on and if you need help. This way he can make sure he helps the people who are behind AND has the necessary things ready for the people working ahead.

Please don't ASK QUESTIONS on this form, ask Mr. Miller directly.

* Required

Name *
First & Last

Class Period *
○ 2nd
○ 3rd
○ 7th
○ 8th

What step number will you be working on at the beginning of this period? *
include only the number (no # symbol or the word "step")

Is there anything you need to tell Mr. Miller about what you're doing?
for example - I'm almost done with this . . . or . . . I'm skipping Step 9 so that I can work on Step 10 with Tommy . . . or . . . I'm supposed to be on Step 12, but have to get materials from at home, so I'm doing Step 13 today.

Each period, when my students entered the classroom, the first thing they did was fill out this Form. Then, they moved on with their work. After greeting my students and taking attendance, I would open up the spreadsheet of results and begin prioritizing the actions I would take during that class period. Let's look at some of those actions with a set of responses from an actual class.

Student 1

As you can see in the image, this student needed assistance. Many middle schoolers, like Anita, may not be willing to (or comfortable enough to) raise their hand to ask for help but are completely comfortable asking for it in this format. After reviewing the form responses, I knew that my first step would be to help this student.

Student 2

This student was way behind the pace of his or her classmates. While this is okay since it's a student-paced course, the form response told me I should check in with this learner. Knowing this, I could update my plan: support Student 1 and then check in with Student 2.

Students 3 and 4

As you can see from the screenshot, some students did not need my help but deserved my praise. Check out the comments from these two students!

- The first says, "[I am] skipping step fifty because I forgot my phone and still have to upload the video to Youtube."

- The second says, "I'm skipping the makey makey [activity] because I need stuff from home that I don't have."

If you've worked with middle schoolers, you know how proud I was that these two students not only took ownership of their mistakes (forgetting necessary items at home) but took appropriate steps (communicating the mistake and moving on to the next activity) to make up for their mistakes. They deserved, and would receive, a compliment for this. With this information, my new plan was to help student 1, check in with student 2, and then praise students 3 and 4.

Student 5

In the image, you can see that this student is way ahead of all of the other students. Most of the students are at or around Activity #49, and this student is at Activity #65. Why would this be important for me to know? I had not made Activity #66 yet!

And that's okay! In a student-paced course, you just need to stay one activity ahead of your students. I was building the plane as I flew it. Keeping track of where all of my students were allowed me to decide when I needed to focus on preparing for the next activity. In this circumstance, because my students had ownership of their own progress, I could actually use some of the class time (after checking in with Students 1–4, from above) to prepare Activity #66.

This all started with a need to know where each student was at the beginning of every lesson. Did my use of this Google Form address that need? For the most part, yes. Within a few minutes of the bell, I knew what each student was working on, and was able to prioritize the students who needed my assistance.

However, as I pointed out at the beginning of this chapter, even after taking these steps, there was still room for improvements. Adding this Google Form solved one set of issues and allowed the opportunity to identify others.

This reminds me, again, of a quote I shared earlier:

Do the best you can until you know better and then when you know better do better.—Dr. Maya Angelou

Before the "Anita event," I had not realized I needed that Google Form. Once I became aware of that (*knowing better*), I was able to solve it (*doing better*). It wasn't that I was doing poorly before this (I had developed a student-paced course, after all!); it was just that I was doing *better* now.

When we discuss the next problem in the next chapter, you will see how it's a continual *know better–do better* cycle.

There's also a little hidden bonus I've alluded to a few times already. It's almost like it's a *know better–do better–do better* cycle. Why? Well, in this situation, my intent was to know what all of my students were working on and know who needed my support. Not only did it do that—the first *do better*—but it also helped me recognize trends in individual students' progress throughout the quarter and provided me with great data for discussions with my students or their parents. There was an additional *do better* level.

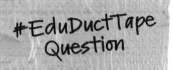
#EduDuctTape Question

How can I track student progress and manage students' questions in a student-paced format?

Online Resource Hub—EduDuctTape.com/hub/chapter10

Decide: Is this #EduDuctTape question (above) one I need the answer to?

☐ **YES!** Continue below. ☐ **NO!** Skim, if you'd like, then move on to the next chapter.

▶ **Think:** What would the ideal tool for tracking student progress and managing students' questions look like **for me, my students, my classroom,** and **my content**? What does it need to do?

_____

_____

_____

_____

_____

▮ MY STRATEGY FOR TRACKING STUDENT PROGRESS

As you read above, my strategy was a Google Form. If you're a Google Workspace for Education user, this is a great option. It's free and it's built into the ecosystem you already use. The way the answers go into a Google Sheet for viewing, analyzing, and keeping data for your records is fantastic.

I should also share a few tips I learned from this experience.

First, I had developed my own system in which, after following up on all of the results for one period, I would hide those spreadsheet rows. This way the records were still there if I needed them, but my view was kept uncluttered. To do this, highlight the rows you want to hide, right-click and select *hide rows*.

Second, data in a Google Sheet can be sorted, even if it came from a Google Form. Sometimes, I would highlight the rows from the current class period, right-click, and select *sort range*. This would allow me to sort by the activity they were on so I could quickly see the distribution of my students' progress.

Third, data in a Google Sheet can also be filtered, even if it came from a Google Form. If I was meeting with a student or a parent, I would often unhide all of the rows and filter the data to only show that student's progress. This way, I could quickly see any trends in their progress or how often they asked for support within the form. To do this, I would highlight all of the data, and select *Data > Create a filter*. Then, click the filter button at the top of the row that shows the students' names. After that, click *clear* under *Filter by values* and then click the specific student's name to only show his or her information.

Fourth, you can add content into the cells to the right of the Google Forms entries. That means that, in my previous screenshot, I could have added observational notes to Column F that correlate to the student's entry in that row. Add that to the sorting and filtering mentioned above and you've got more than just a system for students to ask questions.

Microsoft Forms

Yup, if you can do it in Google Forms, there's a pretty good chance that you can do it in Microsoft Forms. Let's compare Google and Microsoft's question types.

First, both tools offer the following:

- Multiple Choice
- Checkboxes or Multiple-Select
- Dropdown
- Short Answer Text
- Long Answer Text
- Linear Scale
- File Upload
- Date

Google Forms also offers these features:

- Multiple Choice Grid, which Microsoft users could mimic with the Likert option
- Checkbox Grid
- Time

Microsoft Forms also offers these:

- Star Rating, which Google users could mimic with a linear scale
- Ranking
- Likert, which Google users could mimic with a multiple choice grid
- *Net Promoter Score*, which typically asks, "How likely is it you would recommend us to a friend or colleague?," but could be modified. Google users could mimic with a linear scale.

So, as you can tell, the two tools are pretty similar, which means you can use them interchangeably. Similar to how Google Forms results go into Google Sheets, Microsoft Forms results go into Microsoft Excel. In a Microsoft for Education school, you could do the same thing I did with Microsoft tools.

Google Slides or Microsoft PowerPoint

As I mentioned in Chapter 9, one option for a student-paced course would be to organize the course in your slideshow tool, with one slide for each activity. In terms of tracking students' progress, the nice feature here is that, in both Slides and PowerPoint, you can quickly see which slide each student is on because a small icon shows what viewers (or editors) are on each slide. You would immediately know which students were ahead of or behind the pace. You would not, however, see any questions from them unless you handled this in a different manner. You also would not be able to track any progress data over a series of class periods.

Google Classroom or Microsoft Teams

In your basic learning management systems, it's obviously possible to create a student-paced learning experience. Because you can see the assignments your students have submitted (or have not submitted), you'll be able to check their progress. Where this strategy is lacking, however, is the quick snapshot of my entire class I was getting from my spreadsheet. That's not really an option in Google Classroom.

The same will be true in other tools we discussed in Chapter 9. Although tools such as Wakelet, Flipgrid, Seesaw, Google My Maps, websites, or text documents all have merits for housing student-paced coursework, they won't provide you with a great way to see a quick snapshot of students' progress.

> **A reminder:** There is no single correct tool for any of these Educational Duct Tape questions. There is, however, a best tool for *you*. Think about what features and pedagogical outcomes are essential for you and let that guide your selection.

Schoology

Earlier, I gushed about how much I love Schoology's *Student Completion Rules* feature and how well it would fit in a student-paced course. The same is true here. If you create a student-paced course in Schoology, it does a good job of showing your students' progress through it. By clicking on the *Student Progress* button, next to each student's name you will see either a green checkmark that indicates they've done all of the requirements, or a percentage that indicates how many of the requirements they have completed.

Eduflow

Like Schoology, Eduflow's learning experience platform lets you see each of your students' progress through the course materials. In Eduflow, you are presented with a table that shows your students in the vertical column, course activities in the horizontal column, and students' progress (*complete*, *not completed yet*) or even scores or metadata within the main section of the table.

Spreadsheets

It's no secret I love spreadsheets. It's also no secret spreadsheets would be a great option for tracking your students' progress through a student-paced course. In my original solution, students communicated their progress in a Google Form, and I then looked at the results in a Google Sheet. Another option is to leave out the Form and just use the Sheet!

An exemplar of this strategy is a system built by Stephanie Howell (@MrsHowell24 on Twitter), an Instructional Tech Coach in Ohio. In Stephanie's spreadsheet, each student is able to edit the spreadsheet to report their progress to you. You have to give your students edit access to the spreadsheet, but you can set up cell protections so they can only edit their own row of the sheet. It's important to note that students can actually get around these protections, but with a good digital citizenship discussion, you should be okay.

> **You can check it out here:**
> eduducttape.com/howellspreadsheet

In Stephanie's system, your students report three things. First, they have a dropdown box by their name where they can communicate their status—*I'm good, I need help,* or *Check me!*—so you know who needs assistance. Second, they have a dropdown box underneath each assignment where they communicate their status on that assignment—*I'm working* or *Finished*—or leave it blank to show they're not to that assignment yet. Finally, there is a dropdown box for their location so they can communicate if they are out of the classroom and, if so, where they are.

One of the best parts of Stephanie's system is her use of conditional formatting. When your students select *I need help* or *Check me!* the cells automatically highlight red or orange, respectively, so you can quickly see these responses. When selecting *I'm working* or *Finished,* the cells automatically highlight blue or green, which, again, helps you quickly see where all of your students are.

Stephanie's system actually hits on both parts of this Educational Duct Tape question: **tracking student progress** and **managing students' questions**. Let's now look at an option that focuses on the second part of this question.

ClassroomQ

Look, Mom, I found a word that has a Q in it where it's not followed by a U!

Well, that might not be quite accurate, because the Q in *ClassroomQ* could actually refer to two different words—*question* and *queue*—that both include those old buddies *q* and *u*. ClassroomQ was designed by two educators—Kyle Niemis and Dan Martinho—to handle both of those *q* words.

ClassroomQ is like a digital version of the tickets at the deli counter, except for your classroom. Students click *Assistance Needed* whenever they have a *question* to ask. ClassroomQ then places the student into a *queue* while they wait for your help. So, rather than sitting with their hand raised or yelling your name, your students see their place in line and know how long they'll need to wait.

On your end, you'll see that queue—showing the order your students requested assistance—as well as any comments your students included with their request. You can then move through the queue and remove students as you respond to their questions.

ClassroomQ, like most tools, has free and paid versions. The free version gives you enough to get by but limits you to five students in the queue. If you think you might need more, you may need to consider upgrading to a paid version, which adds in some other features, such as seeing which students have joined the class session, live updates of how many times each student has requested assistance, and data from your sessions.

DECISION TIME!

Are you going to try out one of these tools? ☐ Yes ☐ No

Which one(s)?

☐ Google or Microsoft Forms   ☐ Spreadsheets
☐ Slides or PowerPoint   ☐ ClassroomQ
☐ Classroom or Teams   ☐ Something else:_____
☐ Schoology

When are you going to try it out?

☐ Do Now   ☐ Do Soon   ☐ Do Later

Is there a certain lesson, activity, topic, or unit you'll use it for?

_____

_____

If it might solve a problem or meet one of your goals, it's worth committing to trying it out!

Don't forget to check out the resources and tutorials at the Online Resource Hub! There's probably a video about using the tool that you've selected!

EduDuctTape.com/hub/chapter10

ELEVEN

PANICKED TEENAGERS, DUE DATES, AND CALENDARS

Know Better. Do Better.

Part of *knowing* better is being aware of the available technological tools: simply knowing what tools are out there, what they do, and how they can be used. The other part, I believe, is being aware of what's happening in your classroom and reflecting on the things you're observing.

Doing better, then, is making informed decisions based on what you know and, more importantly, taking action on it.

As I mentioned in Chapter 10, my STEM class continued to move through a know-better–do-better cycle. First, I realized my teacher-paced course was the catalyst of a rash of student behavior issues. Then, I resolved it with a student-paced course. Second, I realized I needed an efficient way to be aware of what students were doing each day so I could provide the necessary support as soon as possible. I resolved that with a Google Form on my website. What happened next?

When the first student made the comment, I didn't think much of it. But when I heard the comment from multiple students, I knew something was up.

"Mr. Miller, I'm feeling really stressed out about your class."

Moderate stress can be healthy and improve learning, but I didn't want to expose my students to unnecessary stress. So, I asked questions to figure out what was causing the stress. I can remember one student's response:

Student: "I'm only on activity eight in your class."

You see, even though the students were permitted to move at their own pace in my course, I still expected them to complete a minimum number of activities before the end of the grading period.

Me: "That's actually great! You're only required to finish forty activities in the quarter!"

Student: "I know! That means I have thirty-two activities left to go! That's, like, so many!"

Me: "Well, yes, but you're on activity eight after four days, and there are forty-one days left in the course!"

Student: "Oh man, I don't know if I'll be able to get it all done!"

Me: "But, proportionately, if you've done eight activities in four days, you'll hit forty activities in like twenty days!"

Student: "Pro-por-tion-ate-ly?"

Me: ". . ."

Although the student in this situation was clearly being irrational (they were completing work at a great pace), there was nothing I could do to change a middle schooler's tendency to irrationality. I could tell them their pace was just fine until I was blue in the face, but I couldn't change their tendency to worry that it was not. And I certainly did not want my students worrying.

Let's review our situation here:

- Event: Some students are feeling worried they will be unable to finish their required work on time.
- Ideal Outcome: I wanted all students to know, for sure, where they were in relation to the minimum pace: ahead of it, on it, or behind it.
- Response . . .

I was always willing to tell my students how they were progressing and whether they were on pace, but I wanted them to have ownership over this process. So I added another piece to the website. It already had the activities and a Google Form. Now for element #3.

I embedded a Google Calendar at the bottom of the web page. On the calendar, I listed what day they should finish each activity to stick with that minimum pace. I based the calendar on how long each activity should take. I then added that calendar to the bottom of the webpage, so it was always there and visible to students.

If a student was on Activity 8, like the student above, and they looked on the calendar and saw that on that day they should be completing Activity 4, they would know they were ahead of the pace and need not stress. If they were only on Activity 3, however, they would know they were a bit behind and needed to catch up. And they would, hopefully, take responsibility for planning time to catch up.

It worked. Now I had minimized the behavior problems (thanks to the student-paced site), I was aware of which students needed my support (thanks to the Google Form), and finally, my students were aware of how their progress related to the minimum required pace (thanks to the Google Calendar). My Response (the Calendar) had taken me from my Event (stressed students) to, once again, my ideal Outcome (the stress levels were reduced).

I mentioned earlier the *know-better–do-better–do-better* idea—the idea that when we use technology to solve a problem, we find that it solves that problem, but also addresses problems or goals that we did not know we had. This Google Calendar embedded on my website gave kids further ownership of their progress and more responsibility for their work. Now, not only were my students responsible for the pace at which they were completing work, but they were responsible for identifying when they needed to put in extra time. That responsibility had always been there, but with the addition of the calendar, I had given them the necessary tool for owning that responsibility.

Being impressive is not the goal. Being effective is.

I doubt anyone would call using Google Calendar impressive. Some people might be impressed I embedded it onto a Google Site. Because you've read about my other uses of Google Sites in previous chapters, you're probably not impressed by that either.

If I asked you, however, was my use of Google Calendar in this story *effective*? I'm confident your answer would be *yes*.

If you've interacted with any teacher communities on social media lately, you may have forgotten that effectiveness rather than impressiveness is the goal. A large number of people are sharing impressive things online. Heck, I'm guilty of it too. And it's obviously okay to be impressive. When we do something impressive, we deserve to share about it! What's not okay is for that to be our *goal*.

Every time we use educational technology, there is a temptation to choose the most impressive tool. The *Oxford Learner's Dictionary* defines impressive as "Evoking admiration through size, quality, or skill; grand, imposing, or awesome." I would like to point out a few key words there: *admiration*, *grand*, and *awesome*. It's wonderful when our lessons and technology integrations are *awesome*. It's great when they're *grand*. When a coteacher, colleague, or observing administrator feels *admiration* for our edtech use, that's nice too.

Actually, educators working hard to implement new tools into their classrooms are certainly deserving of admiration; focusing on attaining that admiration is a slippery slope. Attaining admiration or creating awe are great when they happen, but risky when they're our goal.

Our goal in planning lessons or activities cannot be to impress others.

We should have one overarching goal when we plan: being effective. The word *effective*'s origin is the Latin word *efficere*, which means "to accomplish."

Being impressive is not the goal. Being effective is.

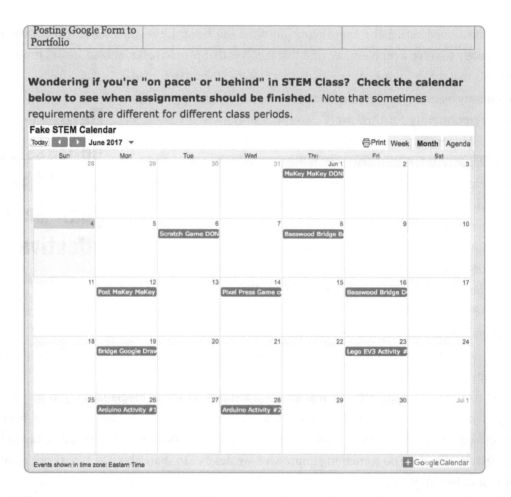

What are you trying *to accomplish* in today's lesson? Is it student ownership? Student retention of a set of vocabulary words? Formative assessment? Comprehension of the rock cycle? Student appreciation of poetry? Hearing every student's voice? What are you trying *to accomplish*?

I was trying to accomplish reducing student stress and informing them of their place in relation to my minimum required pace.

I did not need to be impressive; I only needed to accomplish what I had set forth to accomplish. The *Oxford Learner's Dictionary* defines *effective* as "Successful in producing a desired or intended result."

That should be at the top of our lesson plan books: be "successful in producing a desired or intended result."

What does this mean for us as educators? First, it tells us we need to identify our desired or intended results. Next, we need to plan out how we will determine whether we were successful in producing those results.

If your goal is *impressiveness*, measuring that is easy. The signs of impressiveness are clear. *Oohs, aahs*, high fives, thumbs up, pats on the back, verbal praise. It's easy to know whether people are impressed.

But that is not our goal. Our goal is *effectiveness*. And the signs of effectiveness can be a little more subtle. It's not impossible to measure effectiveness but doing so requires intentionality.

By identifying our *desired or intended result* before we identify our technology, we give ourselves the necessary information to identify our measure of effectiveness. Did we *accomplish* that *result*?

Was my use of Google Calendar effective? My intended results were decreased student stress, increased student responsibility, and an increased number of students working "at or above pace." I was able to measure these things and confirm I accomplished those desired or intended results. Therefore, it was effective.

Being impressive is not the goal. Being effective is.

Ironically, although using Google Calendar is not impressive and embedding it into a Google Site is only slightly impressive, I think the way I used it *was* impressive!

Why? Because it met my goal. Because it accomplished my desired result. Because it was effective. Effective uses of educational technology *are* impressive.

"It's important to keep in mind that," as technology integration coach Dan Stitzel once said in a #EduDuctTape Twitter chat, "being an effective teacher *is* impressive."

Let impressiveness be a byproduct of effectiveness. Focus on your intended result. Aim for effectiveness.

Enjoy the spotlight when people are impressed by your effectiveness.

How can I combine formative assessment with instruction?

Online Resource Hub—EduDuctTape.com/hub/chapter11

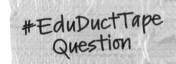
#EduDuctTape Question

■ TOOLS FOR FORMATIVE ASSESSMENT DURING INSTRUCTION

We have discussed formative assessment tools at length. Those tools, for the most part, are nouns for one verb: *assess*. It seems clear that if the tool is truly an assessment **for** learning—meaning it will guide next steps—then it should happen *during* the instructional process. This next set of tools moves the formative assessment into the same platform as the instruction or learning activities by combining multiple verbs: *assess, instruct, inform, deliver content*, and more.

> **Decide:** Is this #EduDuctTape question (How can I combine formative assessment with instruction?) one I need the answer to?
>
> ☐ **YES!** Continue below. ☐ **NO!** Skim, if you'd like, then move on to the next chapter.

▶ **Think:** What would the ideal tool for combining instruction and formative assessment look like **for me, my students, my classroom**, and **my content**? What does it need to do?

_____

_____

_____

_____

Pear Deck and Nearpod

Have you ever had to deal with jealousy between two friends? Like, you went to the mall with your friend Alicia and didn't invite your friend Aaliyah? And Aaliyah is like "Why didn't I get invited to the mall?" (*Even though no one goes to the mall anymore anyhow, so just chill, Aaliyah!*)

The next time you're hanging out with Aaliyah, Alicia is like, "OMG. You're hanging out with her!?"

You just want to tell your friends, "Listen! You're both great! I like both of you!"

Well, Nearpod and Pear Deck are my Alicia and Aaliyah. (I should note: Nearpod and Pear Deck are in no way in the midst of a teenage girl-like competition for my friendship, and I bet they don't even have any animosity toward each other.) They're both fantastic edtech tools. And so what if I want to take Nearpod to the movies and take Pear Deck to play laser tag? Why do I have to pick one? I can be friends with both of them!

At their core, they are very similar: both are instructional platforms that are also great for formative assessment.

Let's start with lesson creation.

In **both** tools, you can do this:

- Build lessons with a combination of content and interactive slides.
- Add text, images, video, audio, and GIFs into slides.
- Use existing templates.

In **Pear Deck**, you can do this:

- Build your lessons within Google Slides or PowerPoint. In Nearpod, most lesson design is done from their website or app, though users in paid plans can use a Google Slides Add-On.
- Create unlimited lessons of unlimited length. In Nearpod, these are both capped, unless you're on the highest of their paid plans.

In **Nearpod**, you can do this:

- Select from many more curated lessons and activities.
- Upload a .pdf, image, or PowerPoint file to Nearpod to Nearpodize it.

Next up, let's look at the interactive features.

In **both**, you can do this:

- Ask multiple-choice questions. In Nearpod, their multiple-choice and true/false quizzes can be autograded or you can set questions as polls.
- Ask text response questions.
- Insert drawing slides where students use pen, line, and text tools to respond. In Nearpod, they can also add images to their responses. In Pear Deck, drawing slides are a premium feature, but you can use a hack (see it in the resource hub!) to add them on free accounts.
- Embed almost any content from the web–websites, articles, YouTube videos, Quizlet flashcards, Jamboards, and more!–within your lessons.

In **Pear Deck**, you can do this:

- Ask number response questions, where the students' answers are compiled onto a box-and-whisker plot.

- Add draggable slides where students drag and place between one and six icons. Like drawing slides, this is a premium feature, but you can use a hack (*see it in the resource hub!*) to add them on free accounts.
  - ▶ A similar feature is available in the paid versions of Nearpod, with the added ability to choose your own images rather than just a collection of icons.

- Set up your slide however you like. In Nearpod, you're limited to their selection of layouts.

In **Nearpod**, you can do this:

- Accept multiple answers in multiple-choice questions.
- Setup multiple-choice and true/false questions as autograded quizzes.
- Allow audio responses in your open ended questions.
- Create *Time to Climb* game versions of quizzes.
- Create drag-and-drop fill-in-the-blank activities.
- Setup *Matching Pairs* activities where students match one text entry or image to another text entry or image.
- Create *Memory Tests*.
- Enable collaborative bulletin board slides called *Collaborate Board Slides*.
- Include PhET interactive simulations (digital science and math simulations).
- Include Microsoft Sways (collaborative canvases or presentations).
- Include Flipgrid topics and see the Flipgrid teacher dashboard on your screen and the student view on the students' screen.
- Add in virtual reality field trips.
- Add in 3-D objects for your students to manipulate.
- Create video activities (we'll discuss this in the next chapter).

Now, let's look at lesson delivery.

In **both** tools you can do this:

- Launch lessons from their site.
- Lead your students through your lesson synchronously (teacher-paced).
- Assign lessons for asynchronous (student-paced) use.
- Switch between teacher- and student-paced during the lesson. In Nearpod, you can set a certain slide for the "student-pacing" to end at.

- Set timers that freeze their screens automatically. In Pear Deck, these can be added and modified during the lesson, while in Nearpod they have to be planned in advance when the lesson is created.
- Present students' responses to the class anonymously and, when appropriate, in views that compile the class data.
- Ask questions on the fly.
  - ▶ In Pear Deck, these can be multiple choice, number, text, drawing, or draggable slides.
  - ▶ In Nearpod, these can be drawing, true or false, open-ended, or website slides.
- See student responses. However, in the free version of Pear Deck, you cannot see which student the responses belong to.

In **Pear Deck**, you can do this:

- Launch lessons from Google Slides or PowerPoint.
- Have unlimited students participate in your lessons. In Nearpod, this is capped to different amounts in each of their levels.
- Freeze students' screens at any point during a teacher-paced lesson. You could mimic this in Nearpod by adding a blank slide.
- View draggable slide responses as an overlay with all responses together.
- View drawing slide responses one-by-one (anonymous, of course) or overlaid on top of each other (this is awesome with graphs in math class!).

> Note that most of these things (PhET simulations, Microsoft Sways, Flipgrid prompts, VR field trips, 3-D objects), can also be included in Pear Deck, but Nearpod does it more efficiently.

In **Nearpod**, you can do this:

- Launch lessons from a mobile app.
- Open up a digital whiteboard to present to your students from.

Finally, let's look at a few key features that the premium versions add to the experience.

Pear Deck offers one paid tier which adds in the abilities to do the following:

- Use draggable and drawing slides (again, you can do it with a hack in the free version).
- Give your students feedback (during or after the lesson) within Pear Deck.

- Generate *student takeaways*—individualized documents shared with each student after the lesson (currently, this only works in Google, not Microsoft).
- Launch single-question *Pear Pops* directly from their Pear Deck page.
- Most importantly, access a teacher dashboard that shows individual student responses during and after the lesson.

Most of the benefits of upgrading to one of the paid versions of Nearpod (*Gold, Platinum, School/ District Premium, School/District Premium Plus*) are actually available in the free version of Pear Deck. Some of the major ones are:

- An increased storage limit
- An increased number of students per lesson
- An increased maximum lesson size
- The addition of a Google Slides add-on for creating lessons
- The ability to have multiple active sessions

Since you're here, reading this chapter, to learn about instructional tools that also offer formative assessment options, we should probably talk a bit about that. Because you can see responses summarized on the projector, both tools are great for quickly checking your class's comprehension as a whole. If you want to see how specific individual students performed, the free version of Nearpod may have a little bit of an edge on Pear Deck. In the free version of Pear Deck, you cannot connect the responses with individual students until *after* the lesson, but in the free version of Nearpod you can do so during the lesson. Also, in Nearpod, you can identify the correct answers to your *quizzes*, and that autograding bonus will give you slightly more useful data for your decision-making. Furthermore, Nearpod provides pretty rich data within your teacher view; in Pear Deck this mostly happens in a spreadsheet.

So, which is better, Alicia or Aaliyah? By now you should know what I'm going to say: it depends on your style, your content, your students, your technology, and your needs. But, it's ap-*pear*-ant that your lessons will be *near*-ly perfect if you add either of the two!

Whiteboard.chat

I think we can all agree 2020 was pretty much the worst year ever. However, a handful of good things came out of that dumpster fire of a year, and most of them were caused by the circumstances. Many educational technology tools grew by leaps and bounds to support education in a pandemic.

Whiteboard.chat literally appeared out of nowhere—at least for me—as a great tool for remote teaching. This free tool's value in a remote or face-to-face classroom makes it a 2020 silver lining. With this tool, do these things:

- ✓ Assign your students to work in individual or group boards.
- ✓ Lead your students through the boards and keep them all on the same slide.
- ✓ Assign boards that are blank or have content loaded (like graph paper grids or blank diagrams) in by you.
- ✓ Create content that includes lots of things, including drawings, text, links, YouTube videos, images, webcam images, background images, and math typing.
- ✓ Add a PDF to your board, with each PDF page on a separate Whiteboard.chat page.
- ✓ Add manipulatives for your students to use, even with an "infinite cloner" option.
- ✓ Select from an available collection of backgrounds and manipulatives.
- ✓ Add timers to your boards.
- ✓ Create boards with a variety of student response options:
  - ▶ Drawings
  - ▶ Text
  - ▶ Links
  - ▶ YouTube videos
  - ▶ Images, including webcam images
  - ▶ Links
  - ▶ Math typing
- ✓ See each student's or group's board.
- ✓ Jump in to collaborate with your students.
- ✓ Respond to your students' requests for help.
- ✓ Showcase a student's work on their classmates' screens.
- ✓ Export your boards as PDFs to do deeper assessments than you might be able to do in the live snapshot.
- ✓ View all of the steps a student took using *Time Machine* mode.

Add in the availability of built-in video and text chatting and the idea that your students will not need accounts to use this tool, and you can see why I consider it a silver lining to the 2020 dumpster fire.

ClassFlow

Have you ever fallen asleep on the couch with the TV on and awakened to a late-night infomercial blaring at you from the screen? You know the one. One of those "But wait! There's more!" infomercials?

ClassFlow is the "But wait! There's more!" of edtech tools. And I don't mean that as a bad thing. Seriously, if Pear Deck and Nearpod are like Google Slides mixed with Formative, then ClassFlow is like all three of them mixed with Google Classroom and Edulastic. It does so many things and, surprisingly, it's free!

- ✓ Use it for formative *or* summative assessments.
- ✓ Use it for standalone assessments *or* lessons.
- ✓ Ask just about every kind of question, including:
    - ✓ Multiple-choice, true/false, and yes or no
    - ✓ Short answer
    - ✓ Math questions
    - ✓ Essay questions
    - ✓ Drawing responses
    - ✓ Matching
    - ✓ Scales
    - ✓ Image labeling
    - ✓ Sorting
    - ✓ Fill-in-the-blank
    - ✓ Choice matrices
    - ✓ *Word seed* polls
- ✓ Project results for your students to see.
- ✓ Look at results from the teacher dashboard.

"And that's not all!" The activities that are a part of ClassFlow are one of the elements that set it apart from other tools:

- ✓ Categorise (*Yes, that is how they spell it. Fancy, right?*)
- ✓ Crossword
- ✓ Flashcards
- ✓ Labeled Diagram

- ✓ Matching
- ✓ Memory Game
- ✓ Sequencing
- ✓ Timeline
- ✓ Venn Diagram
- ✓ Word Search

All the activities can be sent synchronously to your students' devices—like Pear Deck or Nearpod—assigned for your students to use asynchronously or played from a classroom display. ClassFlow works really nicely on a display, which shouldn't come as a surprise because it is from Promethean (an interactive display company), which also might explain why it's available for free.

ClassFlow's presentation capabilities are really cool, too:

- ✓ Lesson cards can be regular presentation slides.
- ✓ Lesson cards can be written on.
- ✓ Lesson cards can contain activities, questions, polls, embedded web content, YouTube videos, embedded files, and more.

Not only can you send the cards to your students' screens like in other tools, but you can also set it to have different cards appear on their screens and your projector screen. Think of your screen showing a video while your students' screens show a question to respond to while watching! I know this is something Pear Deck and Nearpod users would love to have!

I also like the ability to send different cards (or activities) to different students at the same time. Imagine sending a flash cards activity to students who are struggling with a concept and a Venn Diagram activity to those who are grasping the concept a little better. Differentiation built right into your tool!

You may remember I originally referenced ClassFlow as being like a mixture of three tools, one of which was Google Classroom. That's because it has a lot of features that we typically think of being part of a good learning management system, including the ability to do these:

- ✓ Create assignments.
- ✓ Post announcements.
- ✓ Award badges.
- ✓ Store resources.
- ✓ Convert files (Smart Notebook, PDFs, PowerPoints and more!) into ClassFlow activities.

✓ Access premade activities.

The student-facing version is learning management system-like as well: your students can see a *feed* of updates and assignments, revisit activities and materials in their resource area, and more.

As you can tell, ClassFlow has a lot of things going for it. Just as a Swiss Army knife was perfect for my grandfather who wanted to carry around one multifunction tool in his trousers pocket (*Hey, he called them trousers, so I feel like I should too!*), this is a tool for a teacher who wants to learn and manage just one tech tool. Therein lies its one downside: there's a lot to learn in this one tool! Do you *really* need a corkscrew, knife, scissors, and can opener in your pocket? If you do, you might want to call the phone number on that infomercial to buy one of these Swiss Army knives!

Quizizz Lessons

If none of those four amazing options is quite right for you, you might want to check out the Lessons feature in Quizizz. This recent addition to the Quizizz platform is much simpler than the aforementioned tools. Unfortunately, that means your assessment capabilities won't be as extensive. On the bright side, though, it means it's a much less intimidating tool for you if you are not ready for the superpowers of Pear Deck, Nearpod, Whiteboard.chat, or ClassFlow.

✓ Add multiple choice, checkbox, fill-in-the-blank, poll, and open-ended questions.

✓ Include images and math type from the equation editor, just like with regular Quizizz assessments.

✓ Add slides with text, images, videos, or audio.

✓ Annotate your slides with the *Scribble* tool.

✓ Import presentations from Google Slides PowerPoint, or PDFs.

✓ Embed web pages within the lesson.

✓ Use a built in *Spin the Wheel* feature to pick a random student.

DECISION TIME!

Are you going to try out one of these tools? ☐ Yes ☐ No

Which one(s)?

☐ Pear Deck   ☐ Whiteboard.chat
☐ Nearpod   ☐ Quizizz Lessons
☐ ClassFlow   ☐ Something else:_____

When are you going to try it out?

☐ Do Now   ☐ Do Soon   ☐ Do Later

Is there a certain lesson, activity, topic, or unit you'll use it for?

_____

_____

If it might solve a problem or meet one of your goals, it's worth committing to trying it out!

Don't forget to check out the resources and tutorials at the Online Resource Hub! There's probably a video about using the tool that you've selected!

EduDuctTape.com/hub/chapter11

TWELVE

BEARDS, GLASSES, AND HANDSOME TEACHERS

It seems obvious to point out, but since my class had moved to a student-paced blended learning model, it eliminated all of my whole-class instruction and lecture opportunities. This, by the way, reminds me of my favorite quote from the movie *Office Space*. In the scene, Bob Porter, one of the two business consultants known in the movie as "The Bobs," says to the movie's main character, Peter Gibbons, "Looks like you've been missing a lot of work lately."

Peter responds with a smile and a laugh, "Well, I wouldn't exactly say I've been *missing it*, Bob."

I felt similarly about all of the front-of-the-room lectures I was now missing. Much like Peter had replaced his time in his cubicle with time fishing, sleeping in, and dating a character played by movie star Jennifer Aniston, I had replaced much of the time I had spent talking *at* students with time spent talking *with* students.

Sometimes, though, I really was *missing* those whole-class instructional opportunities. I wasn't missing them in the sense of lamenting their absence, rather in the sense of needing to find a new tool for the purpose they served. Sometimes, it was necessary to verbally communicate a set of instructions to all of my students. For those times, I recorded videos and linked them on the Google Site so my students could watch them when they were ready for them.

Sometimes those videos explained essential information; for example, one project in the class was building a basswood bridge (See the image). As part of this project, my students needed to use X-ACTO knives to cut the wood for their

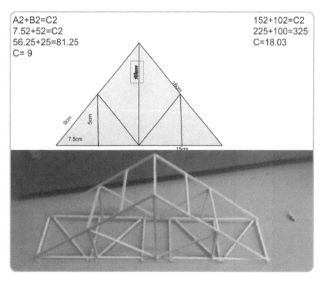

bridge. As you can imagine, when giving thirteen- and fourteen-year-old kids knives to use in the classroom, extensive instructions are necessary. I recorded those instructions in a video along with some other general instructions about the project. One element of the project was that each student and their partner had to plan their bridge by creating a diagram of it in Google Drawings. As you can see from the example drawing, my students not only included the placement of the pieces of wood but also measurements for every piece of wood. I also asked them to include any necessary information for how they calculated those measurements. If they used the Pythagorean Theorem, for example, it was helpful to see that on the screen.

In the original version of this course, I went over these instructions during a (*particularly boring*) whole-class lecture. In this student-paced blended learning format, I needed an alternative method. I provided the instructions for creating this plan in the same video where I went over expectations for using the knives. That meant that there were two reasons that this video was essential viewing for my students.

I can still vividly recall an interaction with a student named Jesse about this very project:

Jesse: "Mr. Miller, I am ready for my wood, glue, and knife."

Me: "Great! Let me look at your plan first."

Jesse: "Plan? What plan?"

Me: "The one I explained in the video. You know, in Google Drawings? With all of the measurements labeled?"

Jesse: "I don't remember anything about a plan."

Me: "Did you watch the video?"

Jesse: "Of course I watched the video."

Me: *Uh, yeah right, Jesse.* (I didn't say that out loud, but wanted to.)

It was pretty obvious to me that he had not watched the video. But I felt like I needed to confirm it.

As you can see from the image above, at the time of the video recording I had glasses and a beard. However, at the time when I had Jesse in class, I had neither. So, I asked him a question:

Me: "What did I look like in the video?"

Jesse: "*Uh* . . . You looked . . . handsome?"

This was obviously not the response I had expected. After laughing at his response (and thanking him), I continued with my line of questioning:

Me: "Thank you for that. But what I meant was, did I look different in any way?"

A classmate attempted to help Jesse by waving his hands and whispering, "Glasses! Beard! Glasses! Beard! Glasses! Beard!"

Jesse, not hearing his friend: "*Uh*, no, you looked pretty much like you do now."

Me: "Did I have glasses in the video?"

Jesse: "No, Mr. Miller, you don't wear glasses."

Me: "Did I have a beard in the video?"

Jesse: "No, Mr. Miller, you don't have a beard."

Me: "In that video, I had both."

It was obvious we both had some work to do. Jesse needed to go back and watch that video. I needed to find a way to make sure my students viewed the videos. It's worth pointing this out again:

$$E \quad + \quad R \quad = \quad O$$

The Event   Your Response   The Outcome

I had no control over the Event (a middle schooler's likelihood to watch a video recorded by their teacher), but I had an Outcome that was important to me (delivering important information to my students). So, I needed to select a Response that would help me reach that outcome.

I could choose from any number of responses.

Making the video more engaging would have probably worked, but focusing on creating viral YouTube-style videos didn't make sense here. It didn't fit the content, the class, or my style as a teacher.

Making the videos shorter and more concise, like my #EduGIFs, may have worked, but it didn't seem to fit this situation. I didn't feel I could trim the video down to a forty-second #EduGIF, and I felt that auditory instructions were important here.

Delivering this information in a face-to-face direct instruction format may have worked, but I felt doing so would undermine the course structure I wanted to build. I was also pretty sure that not all students would pay attention in that format anyhow.

Selecting an edtech response is often a lot like the prewriting process. Through the act of brainstorming, you can clearly define exactly what you need to do. The options I had eliminated helped me clarify my needs and parameters.

I ended up using a tool called EdPuzzle. EdPuzzle allows users to add questions, prompts, and instructions into a video. When those appear on students' screens, the video pauses until they respond. This makes it possible to confirm that students have actually viewed the video. These features made EdPuzzle a great solution for me: when a student like Jesse reported that they were ready for their materials, I could easily confirm whether they had watched the required video.

Remember the *know-better-do-better-do-better* idea I mentioned earlier? Well, it popped up again here:

- *Know Better*—
  - *Know your educational situation:* Middle school students are not likely to watch instructional videos from their teachers.
  - *Know your available technologies:* There's a tool called EdPuzzle that can add questions and prompts into videos and track whether students viewed them.
- *Do Better*—Add my videos into EdPuzzle, add questions, and view the results to confirm that my students were complying.
- *Do Better!*—Here's the unintended bonus for this one. While my intention was compliance-based—confirming that they had viewed the video—my outcome had a second layer: I could formatively assess my students' comprehension!

When a student came up to me for their basswood bridge materials, I was able to do what I intended—confirm they had watched the video—and could do something I hadn't considered—clear up any misconceptions the student may have had when watching the video.

Let's dive deeper into EdPuzzle, and some alternative options, in the next section.

How can I ensure that my students watched required videos and understood the content that they covered?

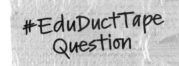

Online Resource Hub—EduDuctTape.com/hub/chapter12

▶ **Think:** What would the ideal tool for adding compliance and assessment into videos look like **for me, my students**, **my classroom,** and **my content**? What does it need to do?

_____

_____

_____

_____

_____

My Strategy: EdPuzzle

I don't know who Ed is and I'm not a big fan of working on puzzles, but I do like EdPuzzle quite a bit. Here are a few things you can do with EdPuzzle:

✓ Use any video on YouTube.

✓ Upload videos that are under 1 gigabyte (GB).

✓ Import videos from Google Drive.

✓ Import videos directly from Screencastify.

✓ Record your own videos using the EdPuzzle Chrome extension.

Once you've selected a video, you'll have access to a variety of features for preparing your video for classroom use, including the following:

✓ Using the *cuts* feature to select a certain portion (or multiple portions) of a video to use.

✓ Adding text or audio *notes* to the video to clarify something or point out something important.

✓ Adding multiple-choice questions.

✓ Adding open-ended questions.

✓ Allow audio responses to open-ended questions.

✓ Including text, equations, and images in your questions and their answers.

What I really love about EdPuzzle is what you see in the teacher dashboard:

✓ Autograded data about your students' performance on the multiple-choice questions

✓ Automatically updated scores for manually graded open-ended responses

✓ Each student's performance

✓ The entire class's performance organized by question

✓ What sections of the video each student watched, as well as whether they repeated any of those sections, a feature that was really useful with Jesse

Like most educational technology tools, EdPuzzle is a "freemium" tool. For a handful of uses, the free plan will give you exactly what you need. If you consider using EdPuzzle regularly, it may be worth considering a paid plan.

PlayPosit

I lied to you. I'm really sorry, but it's true. In the story above, about Jesse and the video? I didn't use EdPuzzle. I actually used Zaption. Zaption was the first tool on the scene to give teachers the ability to embed prompts and questions into a video. I *loved* Zaption. Unfortunately, Zaption left the education market a few years ago when it was acquired by another company. I looked like the "Crying Michael Jordan" meme when this was announced (*go ahead and Google that if you've never heard of it*).

Zaption's departure left teachers to choose between two competing replacements—EdPuzzle and eduCanon. For me, EdPuzzle won. eduCanon later took on the name PlayPosit and is still a tool worth considering, and as you'll soon see, it may meet your needs better than EdPuzzle. With PlayPosit you can do plenty of things:

✓ Combine multiple videos in one *bulb* (their name for their activities).

✓ Use more extensive question options:

    ✓ Multiple Choice or Check All

    ✓ Free Response

    ✓ Fill-in-the-Blank

    ✓ Poll

✓ Add Discussions in which your students type in comments and replies stamped with the correlating time in the video. These discussions can even be active during portions of the video when other questions or prompts appear.

✓ Embed content from the web.

✓ Create screen recordings from within PlayPosit.

✓ Add images and equations to your questions, like in EdPuzzle.

✓ Add audio into your questions.

✓ Add *jumps* into your bulbs to have your students jump over content when their answers prove they get it.

✓ Use *jumps* for student choice too!

With all of those features that aren't part of EdPuzzle, you may be wondering why I referenced EdPuzzle as the tool I use. Honestly, the only downside with PlayPosit is its pricing. There is a free version, but it limits you to only 100 learner attempts per month. Although 100 in a month may be enough for a primary classroom of twenty-five students, it could be problematic for a middle or high school teacher. The free version also prevents you from uploading your own videos to add questions to. As you can tell, it has some features that may make it worth spending the money! With the premium version, you get the ability to do the following:

★ Assign an unlimited number of activities.

★ Upload your own videos.

★ Upload MP3 audio files to turn into activities (only smaller files though).

★ View improved analytics.

★ Deliver *Broadcast Assignments,* in which students respond while you play the video.

★ Allow your students to make their own bulbs.

Nearpod

Uh oh, Aaliyah (Pear Deck) and Alicia (Nearpod) are back! But this time, Alicia is the clear winner. In 2020, Nearpod added a feature Pear Deck doesn't yet have: interactive videos! Nearpod users can now create an EdPuzzle- or PlayPosit-like experience right within Nearpod.

Alicia, *er*—Nearpod lets you upload your own videos or select them from YouTube, trim them, and add open-ended or multiple-choice questions. You can send those videos to your students as is or built into Nearpod lessons. The bonus here is that once the interactive video is added into a lesson, you could also combine it with other videos.

Nearpod's interactive video tool is a bit less robust than EdPuzzle and PlayPosit, but the real bonus here is for teachers who already use Nearpod for lessons. If one tool can do both things, you may not want to use a separate tool for this goal.

Screencastify

In Summer 2021, Screencastify threw its hat into this ring with the announcement that it would soon be adding the ability to add auto-grading multiple choice questions into Screencastify recordings along with the ability to see who views videos. At this point, the details aren't super clear, but two things are: this isn't as robust as the others, but if you're already using Screencastify, it may make sense to consider it!

Wait, that's not all of them!?

If these four tools don't fill the bill for you, there are other options to consider. You could insert your videos and questions into Google Slides and send them in Google Classroom or add videos into Pear Deck slides and ask your questions right there. If you just want to ensure your students are watching the video and thinking about it, using a backchannel chat tool such as BackChannelChat.com or YoTeach! could lead to great discussions during videos. InsertLearning, a tool that lets you add questions into any web content, could also be used to add questions right alongside the video. Your students could use a video note-taking tool like VideoAnt or the ReClipped, YiNote, or Rocket Note Chrome extensions to document their learning.

Finally, it's important to point out that you might not need a video-focused tool to meet this need. Much as you can use Pear Deck or Nearpod here, you can also use any other blended learning tool that works with video. Tools such as TES Teach with Blendspace, Wizer.me, ClassFlow, or even a HyperDoc can be used to combine required videos with strategies for assessing student comprehension.

DECISION TIME!

Are you going to try out one of these tools? ☐ Yes ☐ No

Which one(s)?

☐ EdPuzzle   ☐ Screencastify
☐ PlayPosit   ☐ Something else:_____
☐ Nearpod

When are you going to try it out?

☐ Do Now   ☐ Do Soon   ☐ Do Later

Is there a certain lesson, activity, topic, or unit you'll use it for?

_____

_____

If it might solve a problem or meet one of your goals, it's worth committing to trying it out!

Don't forget to check out the resources and tutorials at the Online Resource Hub! There's probably a video about using the tool that you've selected!

EduDuctTape.com/hub/chapter12

THIRTEEN

TISSUES, DRIPS, AND EIGHT YEARS

As I prepared for writing this book, I spent some time writing down all the funny or memorable stories I could recall. I knew some of these stories would be crafted into anecdotes and become a part of this book. After spending some time doing this on my own, I also asked my kids to try to think of funny stories they remembered. All three of my kids immediately thought of the same story.

This story is accompanied by a video my kids love to watch. The video takes place in a hotel room at the Great Wolf Lodge resort and indoor water park in Sandusky, Ohio. The video shows my daughter Parker, eighteen months old at the time, standing in front of the tissue dispenser in the room. It was built into the front of the sink counter, giving her perfect access.

In the video, Parker pulls out the tissues, one by one, until she is standing in a knee-high pile of tissues. While she determinedly pulls them out, one at a time, my three-and-a-half-year-old son, Cohen, belly laughs in the background. The school psychologist (my lovely wife, April) and I were too tired from the day to stop her.

I love the sound of my son's laughter in the video, but my favorite part is actually at the end of the video. When the tissue box is finally empty, Parker looks down at the floor for the first time and is surprised to see a large pile of tissues around her. She hadn't realized how many tissues she had pulled out or how big the pile would be because she was simply focused on the next tissue.

Our teaching methods, strategies, procedures, and technology integration develop in a similar fashion. Those evolutions don't happen all at once. We make them in stages, tissue by tissue.

Seth Godin references a phenomenon called *focused persistence*. He says that this is the process of catalyzing change, making a ruckus, or building anything big and doing it "drip by drip."

Godin has one of the most popular and followed blogs of all time. And he pointed out in one of those posts that, "You don't launch a popular blog. You build one." How did he build one? Focused persistence.

Most effective educators don't launch an effective classroom on Day One. (Seriously, on my first day, I introduced myself to the first student through the door with my first name. "Hi, I'm Jake.")

Effective educators build an effective classroom much like Godin built a popular blog. He has released a post every day since 2008! He persisted, even when it was difficult or inconvenient. That's focused persistence. Educators who become effective educators do the same thing; they show up and do their best work, every day.

Let's think about that in relation to our craft as educators. As you can tell, I am proud of the STEM class I used to teach. We used technology in lot of impressive ways (a website, a Google Form, a Google Calendar, videos, use of EdPuzzle, etc.), but I did not add those tools all at once. I never could have pulled that off.

Instead, it happened one step at a time. Drip by drip, as Godin says. It happened through focused persistence.

First we developed the vision of the curriculum. Drip.

Then some of the activities. Drip.

Then I realized that in my class students should be able to move at their own pace. Drip.

Then I built the website. Drip.

I identified what I thought was the cause of the behavior problems. Drip. I knew better. Drip. I realized a student-paced course on a website could be the solution. Drip. I did better. Drip.

When I built the site, I didn't put all of the activities on it. Why not? Because they weren't all ready to go onto it yet. So I put them on one by one. Drip by drip by drip.

And when the class started that next quarter, I probably only had three or four activities on the site. I only needed to stay ahead of my students. As long as I was one day ahead of them, I was in good shape. Drip. A day later, drip. And another day later, drip.

And after a while, I realized I had some issues. I needed to know where each kid was in the progression of the course at any given time as well as if they needed my help. So I added a Google Form. Drip.

I knew better. Drip. I did better. Drip.

And then I realized some of my students were overwhelmed by the amount of work they had to accomplish throughout the course of the class. Drip. So, I added a calendar, to keep them aware of where they should be. Drip.

Know better, do better. Drip.

Later, I discovered my students weren't consistently watching the videos that were part of the course. Drip. So I embedded the videos into EdPuzzle so I could be sure they had watched them while also giving my students the opportunity to self-assess and giving me the opportunity to formatively assess. Drip.

Drip by drip.

Drip by drip, I built an impressive class. But those drips were not selected because they were impressive. They were selected because they were effective at producing a desired or intended result. One at a time, drip by drip. Striving for effectiveness through focused persistence.

Drip by drip. Tissue by tissue. One step at a time.

In her book, *Tech With Heart*, high school math teacher turned Director of Innovation and Educational Technology Stacey Roshan talks about her highly impressive flipped high school math classes. She points out that she did not do this all at once. She built this flipped class over the course of eight years! Not all at once but year by year, lesson by lesson, video by video, day by day. Drip. Drip.

In her book, she says, "Making a major change to your teaching practice doesn't happen overnight. That was true for me when I started flipping my classroom. . . . I want you to see that shifting to a flipped model can be a gradual process that improves as you learn what works and what you want to see more of in your classroom." Stacey then expands on what she did during each year of this process in her classroom. Drip by drip. Or, from the perspective of my daughter, tissue by tissue. Focused persistence.

Identify the things that you want to achieve in your class to benefit your students. What are your verbs? What is that Outcome that you desire? You'll likely end up with one big goal or a bunch of goals. Break them apart. Choose your priorities. Identify what step comes first. Set the rest aside for now and focus on your first priority.

The next step is straightforward enough: start.

And the next step? Just as straightforward, but a bit more challenging: persist.

> "STREAKS REQUIRE COMMITMENT AT FIRST, BUT THEN THE COMMITMENT TURNS INTO A PRACTICE, AND THE PRACTICE INTO A HABIT. HABITS ARE MUCH EASIER TO MAINTAIN THAN COMMITMENTS."
> —GODIN

As you move forward, continue to reflect. Do so from the lens of those focuses that you identified. Were the steps that you took effective? You'll get there. And on the way, you'll hit lots of awesome milestones. Celebrate them! And then continue moving forward.

Seth Godin says, "Streaks require commitment at first, but then the commitment turns into a practice, and the practice into a habit. Habits are much easier to maintain than commitments." Make your commitment now, and it'll be your habit later.

Participate in the Adjacent Possible and share your takeaways with other Duct Tapers: EduDuctTape.com/hub/chapter13

Thanks for reading *Educational Duct Tape: An EdTech Integration Mindset.*

I've got a little quiz for you! Grab your pencil!

- ☐ Did you laugh at least once while reading it?
- ☐ Do you feel more equipped to integrate technology?
- ☐ Did you learn some new stuff?
- ☐ Will this experience benefit your students?
- ☐ Do you want to see your colleagues grow as edtech integrators, too?
- ☐ Do you want to see their students' experiences improve?
- ☐ Do you want some free Educational Duct Tape swag?
- ☐ Will you do me a favor?

If you checked all of those boxes, follow this simple two-step process!

- ✓ Review the book on Amazon, GoodReads, or another book reviews platform.
- ✓ Head to eduducttape.com/reviewswag to claim your free swag bundle!

BIBLIOGRAPHY

Custom app, platform, and website designs featured in this book were created by Monica Isabel Martinez (mpowerPL), bit.ly/mpowerdesigns

Chapter 1

DITTO, Inc, et al. "A Ditto Magazine Ad from 1954 and a Homework Sheet from 1970." *MULTIMEDIAMAN*, 22 Nov. 22, 2014, multimediaman.blog/2014/11/22/albert-blake-dick-1856-1934.

Hyperstudio Multimedia CD image. *EBay*, 27 Sept. 27, 2019., ebay.com/itm/Evaluation-CD-Hyperstudio-Multimedia-by-Roger-Wagner-1993-1998-CD-ROM-Win-Mac-/264477665986.

Jenkins, Thomas. "Oregon Trail Screenshot." *Medium*, 19 May 19, 2017, link.medium.com/0EkjUjlGSdb.

"SMART Board 580." *TechEdu*, Interworld Highway, LLC, www.techedu.com/Smart_580.asp.

Tetrault, Gregory. "PowerPoint's Tri-Pane View." *ATPM: An e-Zine about the Personal Computing Experience.*, ATPM, Inc., 2001, www.atpm.com/7.01/office.shtml.

"Where in the World Is Carmen Sandiego?" *Games Info DB*, My U, www.gamesinfodb.com/game/where-in-the-world-is-carmen-sandiego.

Chapter 2

E, F (faizedzahar). "Ilmu baru di Google Sheet hari ini. Sebarkan untuk manfaat semua." 28 Mar. 2019, 1:59 AM. Tweet.

Mk4rim. "Using Google Sheets to translate batches of words. Great for language learning." 1 Apr. 2019. reddit.com/r/lifehacks/comments/b81zqh/using_google_sheets_to_translate_batches_of_words. 14 Feb. 2021.

Chapter 3

Wiliam, Dylan. "Formative Assessment: Getting the Focus Right." *Educational Assessment* (2006).

Gimkit. "Gimkit." gimkit.com. Accessed 18 February 2020.

Hattie, John. "Hattie Ranking: 252 Influences and Effect Sizes Related to Student Achievement." *Visible Learning*, March 28, 2018, visible-learning.org/hattie-ranking-influences-effect-sizes-learning-achievement/. Accessed February 15, 2021.

Hattie, John. *Visible Learning*, 1st ed. Oxforshire, England: Routledge; 2008.

Hattie, John. "Visible Learning Plus 250+ Influences on Student Achievement." visible-learning.org/wp-content/uploads/2018/03/250-Influences-Final-Effect-Size-List-2017_VLPLUS.pdf.

Chapter 4

Formative. "Formative." *Formative*, 2021, goformative.com. Accessed 14 May 2021.

Schwartz, Barry. (2006) More Isn't Always Better. *Harvard Business Review* (2006). hbr.org.

Schwartz, Barry. "The Paradox of Choice." *TED: Ideas Worth Spreading*, July 2015, ted.com/talks/barry
_schwartz_the_paradox_of_choice.

Chapter 5

Hattie, John. "Hattie Ranking: 252 Influences and Effect Sizes Related to Student Achievement." *Visible Learning*, March 28, 2018, visible-learning.org/hattie-ranking-influences-effect-sizes-learning
-achievement. Accessed February 15, 2021.

Hattie, John. *Visible Learning*. 1st ed., Oxfordshire, England: Routledge, 2008.

Hattie, John. "Visible Learning Plus 250+ Influences on Student Achievement." *Visible Learning Plus*, Nov. 2017.

Oravec, J. A. "Bookmarking the World: Weblog Applications in Education; Weblogs Can Be Used in Classrooms to Enhance Literacy and Critical Thinking Skills." *Journal of Adolescent & Adult Literacy*, 45, no. 5 (2002): 616-621.

Fink, Lisa. "Teaching with Blogs." *NCTE*, Nov. 3, 2019, ncte.org/blog/2019/11/teaching-with-blogs.

"Reflective Practices as Embedded Instructional, Cultural Design." *PBLWorks*, Buck Institute for Education, my.pblworks.org/resource/blog/reflective_practices_as_embedded_instructional_cultural_design.

Agarwal, Pooja K. "What is retrieval practice?" *Retrieval Practice*, 2019. retrievalpractice.org/why-it-works.

W3Techs. Usage Statistics of Content Management Systems. *W3Techs Web Technology Surveys*, Q-Success, 15 February 2021. w3techs.com/technologies/overview/content_management.

Chapter 6

McMillan, James H, and Hearn, Jessica. "Student Self-Assessment: The Key to Stronger Student Motivation and Higher Achievement." *Educational Horizons*, vol. 87, no. 1 (Fall 2008): 40-49. EJ815370. *ERIC*, files. eric.ed.gov/fulltext/EJ815370.pdf. Accessed February 15, 2021.

Hattie, John. *Visible Learning*. 1st ed. Oxfordshire, England: Routledge, 2008.

Hattie, John. " Hattie Ranking: 252 Influences and Effect Sizes Related to Student Achievement." *Visible Learning*, March 28, 2018, visible-learning.org/hattie-ranking-influences-effect-sizes-learning
-achievement/. Accessed February 15, 2021.

Carlson, Will (MrCarlsonsClass). "Umm so my students just asked for vocabulary review with @gimkit during recess. Please advise." 18 Oct. 2018, 9:51 AM. Tweet.

Cooney Horvath, Jared. *Stop Talking, Start Influencing: 12 Insights from Brain Science to Make Your Message Stick*. Dunedin: Exisle Publishing; 2019.

Chapter 7

Screencastify. "Screencastify | The #1 Screen Recorder for Chrome." *Screencastify*, 2020, screencastify. com. Accessed 18 February 2020.

Farah, Kareem. "Everything You Need to Know about Building a Great Screencast Video." *Cult of Pedagogy*, Building Modern Classrooms Project, Apr. 26, 2020, cultofpedagogy.com/screencast-videos.

Chapter 8

Godin, Seth. "Falling Out." *Seth's Blog*, Feb. 1, 2018, seths.blog/2018/02/falling-out/.

Clark, Holly. "Assessment Reform in Education During Distance Learning." *Adobe Blog*, Apr. 28, 2020, blog.adobe.com/en/2020/04/28/distance-learning-means-rethinking-assessment.html#gs.t2ivbk.

Wormeli, Rick. The Collected Writings (so Far) of Rick Wormeli: Crazy Good Stuff I've Learned about Teaching. Westerville, OH: Association for Middle Level Education, 2013.

Pink, Daniel H. *Drive: The Surprising Truth about What Motivates Us*. New York: Riverhead Books; 2009.

Enthoven, Julia. "Why We Chose an Onomatopoeia for the Name of Our Startup." *Kapwing Company Blog*, Kapwing, 28 Mar. 2018, kapwing.com/blog/why-we-chose-an-onomatopoeia.

Chapter 9

Hattie, John. "Hattie Ranking: 252 Influences and Effect Sizes Related to Student Achievement." *Visible Learning*, March 28, 2018, visible-learning.org/hattie-ranking-influences-effect-sizes-learning-achievement.

Chapter 11

Cooney Horvath, Jared. *Stop Talking, Start Influencing: 12 Insights from Brain Science to Make Your Message Stick*. Dunedin: Exisle Publishing, 2019.

"Impressive." Oxford Learner's Dictionaries, 2021. *OxfordLearnersDictionaries.com*.

Stitzel, Dan (mr_stitzel). "A2: It's important to keep in mind that being an effective teacher IS impressive. #EduDuctTape" Oct. 9, 2019, 9:37 PM. Tweet.

Chapter 12

Judge, Mike, director. *Office Space*. Twentieth Century Fox Home Entertainment, 1999.

Chapter 13

Godin, Seth. "Streaks." Seth's Blog, August 8, 2019, seths.blog/2019/08/streaks/.

Godin, Seth. "Writer's Block and the Drip." *Seth's Blog*, Dec. 31, 2012, seths.blog/2012/12/writers-block-and-the-drip/.

Roshan, Stacey. *Tech with Heart: Leveraging Technology to Empower Student Voice, Ease Anxiety, & Create Compassionate Classrooms*. San Diego: Dave Burgess Consulting, Inc., 2019.

ACKNOWLEDGMENTS

The Adjacent Possible. I talk about it regularly on my podcast. It is an idea that I first heard in George Couros's book *The Innovator's Mindset.* The concept started with evolutionary biologist Stuart Kauffman and evolved to relevance outside of the science community when Steven Johnson applied it to innovation and ideas.

Kauffman theorized that organisms and their parts evolve through incremental changes. Johnson and Couros both remixed this idea as a way of imagining how ideas evolve and innovation happens.

From my viewpoint, it is the way that our potential is impacted by those with whom we surround ourselves. What is possible for us is determined by what is adjacent to us. I have been fortunate to have been *adjacent* to many amazing people who have expanded my potential.

Here are some of those adjacent individuals:

- Dan Stitzel expanded my ability to implement the Oxford comma. I am grateful, proud, and indebted. Dan's help as an unofficial editor throughout the drafting of this book was helpful, valuable, and impactful. I have been happy to fulfill his payment in the form of a few hazy IPAs. Calling it a bargain is an understatement.

- Heath Blackard also unselfishly gave his time to previewing an early draft of this book. His efforts were unpaid, but I might be able to pay him with money from the banana stand. There's always some there.

- Andreas Johansson gifted me with the book *What To Do When It's Your Turn (and It's Always Your Turn)* by Seth Godin. I've been taking my turn ever since. He also was one of the first to give me a turn presenting in front of educators.

- Karen Moore, Mark Treen, and Randi Armstrong gave me a turn before I even knew I was ready for it as part of a Technology Leadership Team. They were some of my earliest thoughtpartners in my educational technology journey.

- Dr. William Kist once told me, "You should write a book." He was right. He also gave me lots of opportunities and advice.

- Many of the principals and assistant principals that I've worked with have provided me with support and knowledge that helped me on my journey as an educator. Many of them also annoyed me with some of their administrative decisions, but that's okay because if we agree on everything, someone's not thinking.

- David Ternent grew alongside me as our ideas of what STEM education could be grew and evolved. Dave was also kind enough to read an early draft of this book. I'll be repaying him with a free container of my hair product.

- Christa Krohn shared her insights on instructional coaching, has been a great thought-partner, and has always cheered me on.

- Ann Radefeld has been a trusted listener and advice provider throughout my journey. I couldn't have selected a better first guest for my podcast.

- Lissa Brunan, Dr. Annette Kratcoski, April Miller, Angela Greene, and Molly Klodor all gave their time to read early drafts of this book and provide varying levels of feedback.

- Jen Giffen provided an amazing set of sketchnotes in support of this book.

- Monica Isabel Martinez created a super cool set of graphics for this book.

- Stacey Roshan unselfishly gave her time to read this book and record a discussion about the book.

- I am honored to have Tony Vincent, Kasey Bell, Matt Miller, Dr. Catlin Tucker, Holly Clark, Eric Curts, Dr. Sarah Thomas, and Dr. Monica Burns listed amongst the individuals who provided endorsements for this book. How cool is that?

- Finally, I have worked on teaching teams with dozens of amazing educators. Some of them helped me grow as a teacher, but all of them helped me hone my sense of humor. I hope that it pays off for the readers of this book.

WANT TO BRING JAKE'S ENERGY AND GOOFY SENSE OF HUMOR TO YOUR SCHOOL OR EVENT?

Visit JakeMiller.net/Speaking for videos and details!

"Thank you for the only PD that I've done that wasn't a waste of time!"

—Attendee, Best Practices & Tools for Learning in All Settings: 4 MVPs @ Virtual Oconee County Summer Institute 2021

"This was exactly what I needed to hear as I'm gearing up for the start of school next week!"

—Attendee, Educational Duct Tape @ Virtual Indiana Connected Educators Conference, 2020

"You are such a pleasure to listen to. I love your podcast, and I love how organized and fun your presentations always are. I've attended your sessions in person and virtually, and you never fail to be FANTASTIC!"

—Attendee, The 4 MVPs of Remote + Blended Learning from a #EduDuctTape Mindset @ Virtual TCCA 2020

"I've been in education for 25+ years and feel like I've heard speakers that all start to sound the same. But you are a light! Thanks for your enthusiasm!"

—Attendee, Educational Duct Tape Keynote @ Virtual Fort Worth ISD Tech Conference, 2021

"I thought it was great—probably the best PD I've done. Your personality and presentation style are also engaging and entertaining."

—Attendee, Best Practices & Tools for Learning in All Settings: 4 MVPs @ Virtual Oconee County Summer Institute 2021

"Your enthusiasm and passion are palpable and inspiring. You're engaging and thorough. Thank you!"

—@athorp, Attendee, The 4 MVPs of Remote + Blended Learning from a #EduDuctTape Mindset @ Virtual Teach with Tech Conference 2021

"Holy Cow, Batman! Love your podcast regularly, but really loved watching you teach! Animated, excitable, and you LOVE your job!"

—Attendee, Holy Sheets! Spreadsheets in the Math Classroom (and beyond) @ Virtual Teach With Tech Conference 2020

"Your message was perfect and just what I needed today."

—Attendee, Flexible Learning with EdTech: Preparing for Back to School @ Virtual Kami Connect Conference 2020

"You continue to inspire me. I appreciate you being real and sharing the insight from your current teaching experience."

—Attendee, Choice Boards in the Classroom @ Virtual Sylvan Union ISD Session, 2021

"I loved how engaging you were. THANK YOU SO MUCH! I absolutely LOVED listening to you."

—Attendee, Holy Sheets! Spreadsheets in the Math Classroom (and Beyond) @ Virtual Teach With Tech Conference 2020

"Thank you for sharing your gifts and talents to help us be better to help our kids."

—Attendee, Educational Duct Tape Continued @ OETC 2020

ABOUT THE AUTHOR

JAKE MILLER is an eighth-grade science teacher, edtech and learning enthusiast, speaker, cheerleader of teachers, and host of the Educational Duct Tape podcast. Jake previously spent five years as a technology integration specialist and an additional thirteen years in the classroom teaching math, science, and STEM at various grade levels. Jake's favorite job, however, is his full-time position as a husband and father.

Made in United States
Troutdale, OR
12/26/2023

16457487R00097